Educational Accountability: The State of the Art

International Network for Innovative School Systems (INIS)

Kenneth Leithwood
Karen Edge
Doris Jantzi

Bertelsmann Foundation Publishers
Gütersloh 1999

Die Deutsche Bibliothek – CIP-Einheitsaufnahme
Leithwood, Kenneth : Educational accountability :
the state of the art/ – Kenneth Leithwood ; Karen Edge ;
Doris Jantzi. – Gütersloh : Bertelsmann Foundation Publ., 1999
  ISBN 3-89204-435-X

© 1999 Bertelsmann Foundation Publishers, Gütersloh
Responsible: Dr. Anne Sliwka, Cornelia Stern
Copy Editor: Sabine Stadtfeld
Production Editor: Christiane Raffel
Cover design: werkzwei, Lutz Dudek, Bielefeld
Cover photo: Mauritius
Typesetting: digitron GmbH, Bielefeld
Print: Fuldaer Verlagsanstalt GmbH, Fulda
ISBN 3-89204-435-X

Contents

Section C: Accountability Policies and Practices in Selected Countries

Acknowledgements

Many people assisted with this study – providing documents, reviewing drafts and collecting interview data. We are extremely grateful to the following people for this assistance:

Steve Benson

Klaus Buhren

Eckhard Buresch

Christoph Burghard

Anne Marie Carrie

Erling Daehlie

Anton de Jong

Olly den Hartogh

Peter Döbrich

Jap Doorn

Professor Dronkers

Fred Feuerstake

Tobias Hagmann

Wolfgang Meyer-Hesemann

Georg Knauss

Mr. Kovacs

Tove Kvil

Harry Liedtke

Stephen MacKenzie

Archie McGlynn

Frans Meyer

Geza Molnar

Barbara Niedrig

Michael O'Neill

Phillipe Perrenoud

David Philips

Wolf Schwarz

Peter Sleegers

Anne Sliwka

Anton Stritmatter

Martin Thrupp

Monica Gather Thurler

Fons van Wieringen

Vilmos Vass

Section A: A Framework for Understanding Educational Accountability

Introduction

Background

Greater accountability sometimes has been advocated for schools and school systems simply as a means of demonstrating to taxpayers that they are getting reasonable value for their educational dollar. More often, however, strategies and tools for increasing the accountability of schools are integral parts of much broader school reform initiatives. In many cases those strategies and tools are the central vehicles for reform, on the assumption that holding schools more accountable for achieving their processes and outcomes will itself trigger improvements unspecified and perhaps unimagined by those advocating such accountability. Indeed, it is not an exaggeration to claim that accountability is the prominent zeitgeist of education in the 1990s and seems likely to remain so well into the next millennium.

The timing of calls for greater accountability on the part of schools and school systems has been remarkably similar across many countries although the reasons for those calls have not always been the same as illustrations from several countries suggest. In the US, calls for greater educational accountability became quite strident in the late 1960s and early 1970s, subsided briefly only to reemerge with much greater energy in the early 1980s. School choice, a central feature of the US accountability movement during the latter part of this period, arose in a political and social context "unlike any other period in American history" (Croninger & Lee, 1995, p. 13). During that time the US underwent a cultural transformation in which values supportive of civic ties and obligations were replaced by values associated with personal acquisition and self-interest. "Although this cultural shift established an environment conducive to choice, the catalyst was the election of Ronald Reagan, which swept into the mainstream of educational policy-making and leadership a chorus of conservative voices that was anti-government and pro-business in pitch (Cookson, 1994, p. 316)."

Concerns giving rise to increased school accountability in New Zealand also began to emerge in the early 1960s. These concerns can be traced to dissatisfaction with progress in changing the school system under a highly centralized administrative structure. By the late 1980s discontent on the part of communities and groups that were disadvantaged by the system, such as Maori and women, could not be ignored. This led the government to restructure its health, education and other departments to achieve smaller, more effective regional units. A new Education Act came into effect in October, 1989. At that time schools took over their own administration, previous regional primary education boards were disestablished, and school Boards of Trustees elected by parents were set up to govern all state schools – primary and secondary (Williams, Harold, Robertson, & Southworth, 1997, Butterworth, S., 1998).

Calls for greater accountability in England grew out of concerns, during the early 1970s over the closed nature of the school curriculum, a curriculum largely decided by teachers with little or no influence by parents, business people or the government. Local educational authorities provided little direct guidance to schools on such matters. In 1976 the chief inspector of schools gave a widely reported speech drawing attention to the problem and the national inspectors' reports began to raise questions about the quality and relevance of what was being taught for the modern world. These and other initiatives eventually culminated in the Education Reform Act in 1988. One part of that Act was concerned with a national curriculum and methods to assess its achievement. The second part of the act focused on the creation of a market system in education based on the philosophy that efficiency and quality are best sustained and enhanced where there is choice and the information needed to make sensible decisions (Williams, Harold, Robertson, Southworth, 1997; Barber, 1996).

According to Weiss (1993), the main source of concern about accountability in Germany was not a diagnosed quality crisis, as in the US, but an attempt to cope with dwindling political legitimation and to reduce educational policy conflicts. These conflicts arose in response to the significant social, political, economic, and cultural changes that occurred in the past two and a half decades. A fiscal crisis challenged the welfare state and caused growing awareness of the limitations of the state's problem-solving capacity. Increased pluralism in the value orientation of society developed in Western Germany in particular and this triggered a "... fundamental discussion about the role of state, about the nature and scope or the state's function that also seized the field of education as criticism of the status quo" (1993, p. 307). Changes, however, were not driven by a desire to introduce market forces, as in England or New Zealand.

Whereas many tools for increasing school accountability, especially those aimed at increasing competition for students, are of relatively recent origin in many countries, this is not the case everywhere. School choice, for example, emerged as a noticeable movement in the 1980s in the US and some other countries. But the Netherlands has been pursuing its own unique version of school choice for more than 60 years. Since the 1920s parents in that country have been able to choose among Catholic, Protestant and religiously neutral, private-sector schools. Furthermore, schools in the Netherlands are financed according to the number of pupils enrolled. So parents dissatisfied with prevailing school options may establish a new school by finding enough parents who will send their children to that school.

With some exceptions, then, the current preoccupation with educational accountability appears to have begun in most developed countries in the 1960s, acquiring significant new energy during the mid-to-late 1980s. The reasons for these calls for greater accountability, furthermore, are to be found in the wider economic, political, and social context of which schools are a part. These contexts are not uniform across all countries. Nevertheless, a core of developed countries including, for example, Australia, New Zealand, the UK, and Canada, have been similarly influenced by the New Right ideology. Peters has described the context of New Right thinking as follows:

"... a universal administrative reform movement precipitated immediately by a fiscal crisis due to two factors: changes in the international economic system and the spiraling demand for government services. This situation has been variously described as the 'crisis of the welfare state' (OECD, 1981), as a breakdown of the Keynesian post-war consensus, and as leading to a global shift to the right in Western capitalist democracies. In general terms, policy responses have aimed first and foremost at greater budgetary restraint pursued in a variety of ways: the downsizing of public-funded organizations; corporatization and privatizing strategies; deregulation; and asset sales programs" (1992, p. 269).

Purposes

Clearly, the forms that accountability may take in schools and education systems, as a whole, need to be better understood as do the consequences of introducing one form as distinct from another need to be better understood. Hence, the general purpose of this paper – to provide a descriptive account of contemporary educational accountability policies and practices evident in a sample of developed countries around the world (examining the consequences of various accountability tools is beyond the scope of this paper).

The concept of accountability

The concept of accountability used in this paper owes much to the insight of Robert Wagner (1995) developed in his book, *Accountability in education: a philosophical inquiry* (New York: Routledge). Liberally adapted for the study, this conception is developed as a response to five issues:
– What level of accountability is to be provided?

- Who is expected to provide the account?
- To whom is the account owed?
- What is to be accounted for?
- What are the consequences of providing an account?

What level of accountability is to be provided?

The starting point for answering this question is the dictionary meaning of the term accountability and its near "relatives." Webster's 7th New Collegiate Dictionary, for example, claims that the quality of being accountable means being subject to giving an account, being answerable, and capable of being accounted for. The term "account" entails giving a report on, furnishing a justifying analysis or explanation, providing a statement of explanation of one's conduct, offering a statement or exposition of reasons, causes, grounds, or motives, or simply providing a statement of facts or events.

These dictionary definitions begin to clarify one of the distinctions central to a more fundamental conception of accountability, the "level" of accountability called for. For example, included within the meaning of "providing an account," according to the dictionary definitions, is the relatively simple description of events. A school which distributes a calendar outlining its program options for students along with other events, policies and the like, that it considers noteworthy for students and parents is "providing an account" in the *descriptive* meaning of the term. For present purposes, this will be considered the simplest or lowest level of accountability.

Also referred to as part of the meaning of account, however, is the more difficult offering of an *explanation* for events. The typical school calendar would not suffice as an account given this meaning of the term, unless added to the calendar was further information about the sources of programs, the reasons for other events, and the like. Such a calendar, however, would still fall short of "providing an account" when the term is defined to include *justification* for events, the highest level of accountability for purposes of this paper. This meaning of "providing an account" would require the calendar to contain not only descriptions and explanations. It also would require arguments of some sort for why these programs and events were the most appropriate ones for the school to be offering its students.

Based on this understanding of levels of accountability, questions useful for describing and comparing accountability policies and practices should include:
- Is the account to be a description of purposes and/or activities?
- Is the account to be an explanation of purposes and/or activities?
- Is the account to be a justification for purposes and/or activities?

Who is expected to provide an account?

"Responsibility" is one of two minimum conditions for validating the assignment of any accountability obligation and whatever interpersonal relationships it may entail, according to Wagner's (1995) analysis. The assignment of any responsibility or obligation to provide an account is usually contingent upon identifying the person or parties responsible for the act creating it. This depends on the act itself and the institution within which the act is carried out. So, one becomes obliged or responsible to provide an account as a result of either an act that one undertakes or the role that one occupies within an organization.

A person or group can be causally responsible for an act which is self-evident and ultimately personally obliging. This may be an act actually committed by the person or group, as in the obligation a teacher assumes for the welfare of her students on a field trip. Obligations also arise when the person or group exercises influence on others to perform an act. This type of obligation is acquired by a principal for example, in relation to the quality of instruction in a teacher's classroom, when that principal encourages the teacher to implement innovative curriculum material.

Persons or groups may be responsible, as well, for the omission of acts – acts in which the person's or group's engagement is considered inappropriate. The teacher taking students on a field trip to the zoo is expected not to detour through the local shopping plaza en route to the zoo. Such persons or group also may be causally responsible for an act which is initially but not ultimately obligating because of mitigating

14

circumstances. While the teacher is initially responsible for the safety of his students on a field trip, various natural disasters (e. g., lightening or other "acts of God" as the insurance industry calls them) would be considered beyond the teachers control, thus absolving the teacher from responsibility providing that he took appropriate precautions on behalf of his students.

And joint responsibility may be acquired for an act incurring a shared obligation among those responsible. The statutes and laws governing elementary and secondary education in most developed countries, for example, hold teachers and principals jointly responsible for students' educational experiences. Individual or joint responsibility may be acquired for an act obligating others, as well. In some jurisdictions (e. g., the Canadian province of Ontario) principals and superintendents are jointly responsible for the quality of instruction that teachers provide their students.

One acquires obligations not only through the acts one carries out oneself (creating causal obligations) but also through the roles or positions one holds in life: for example, educators historically have been expected to behave in both their personal and professional lives in ways that are consistent with the norms of morality held by the communities in which they work. Such roles create non-causal or "expectational" obligations of either a specific (e. g., what we do as teachers), or general nature (what we are expected to do as good neighbors or citizens). Expectational obligations are in reference to potential acts or performances that are possible to fulfill, consistent with the role from which they are said to derive, and reasonable to expect in light of other considerations that are equally relevant.

Most people have acquired both causal and expectational types of obligations and these types become very difficult to distinguish in real-life circumstances.

It is highly questionable, according to Wagner (1987), whether a person should be held accountable for acts which, causally, he has neither omitted, committed or influenced. It is equally questionable whether a person should be held accountable for expected performances which are impossible to satisfy (e. g., ensuring that all students learn to high standards), are inconsistent with the role from which they are said to derive (e. g., teachers being held responsible for students' use of illegal substances), or whose assignment and satisfaction may be quite unjustified by other factors (principals being held responsible for improving the average reading scores of students in schools with highly transient student populations).

Also it is questionable whether a person or an organization should be held solely accountable for matters involving a shared, causal responsibility. The success of students in school, for example, is a function of many factors. While the quality of teachers' instruction is important, it is significantly influenced by such factors over which the community or the government, not the teacher or the school, has control such as the physical condition of the school building, the size of classes, the time available for teachers to prepare for classes, and the like. In an article making the case for a concept of "community accountability," Henry (1996) describes a relevant example of an attempt to hold schools accountable for actions that clearly entail a shared responsibility at minimum:

> "In Virginia, legislation was proposed to combat hunting-related accidents by requiring all students to participate in the 'hunter education curriculum.' This legislation came as a camouflaged alternative to mandating that hunters wear highly visible, orange attire."

As he claims more generally, "Society deposits its drugs, violence, intolerance, and other problems at the school's doorstep" (p. 87), and holding schools solely or largely accountable for solving such problems violates any reasonable assignment of legitimate responsibility.

Nor is it legitimate to hold a person solely accountable for expected performances requiring a shared influence, unless it is specifically understood that the person is answerable for the actions of others, as would seem to true of parents' responsibility for the actions of their children, or executives' responsibility for the work of subordinates. When we know, for example, that family educational culture accounts for at least 50 percent of the variation in student achievement, how is it possible to claim that schools alone should be held accountable for such achievement?

Based on this position concerning how the responsibility for provid-

16

ing an account is acquired, questions useful for describing and comparing accountability policies and practices should include:
- Is the person or group being asked to provide an account, causally responsible for the act?
- Has the person being asked for the account acquired an obligation through the roles or positions he or she holds?
- Is the act for which accountability is required initially, but not ultimately obligating because of mitigating circumstances?
- Is the person being asked for an account jointly responsible for an act incurring a shared obligation among those responsible?
- Is the person being asked for the account individually or jointly responsible for an act obligating others as well?

To whom is an account owed?

"Entitlement" of the person or group requesting an account is the second minimum condition for justifying such a request. Entitlement is a function of whether a legitimate interest can be shown by those expecting an account. Such an interest must be demonstrated in order to validate an obligation to satisfy an accountability demand.

There are different degrees of entitlement to an account and one's entitlement increases with the degree of valid interest one has in the act for which the account is requested. This is sometimes quite difficult to determine. For example, when a teacher is required to provide an account of their classroom instruction through participation in a performance appraisal process, it seems clear that the appraisee and the appraiser are entitled to the account. But who else might have a legitimate entitlement to the account? Typically, very few others have access to the results of the appraisal (perhaps a senior school system official through the personnel files kept in the school system's office). But what is the entitlement of the parents of the teacher's students, and the students themselves? It does not seem difficult to justify the pre-eminence of their entitlement, although many reasons unrelated to entitlement have been developed to keep formal accounts of teacher performance out of reach of those whose entitlements may be greatest.

Instead, the closest parents and students typically get to a formal account of teacher performance is a report of student achievement and such reports usually are considered to be more relevant to student than teacher accountability. Indeed, this is clearly a flawed basis for teacher accountability since teachers, parents, students, peers, and a variety of physical and social conditions combine in their contribution to student achievement. Responsibility for student achievement is jointly shared, whereas responsibility for teacher performance is much more unambiguously teachers' responsibility.

Given this approach to determining who is owed an account, questions useful for describing and comparing accountability policies and practices should include:
− To whom is the account to be given?
− Do those expecting an account have a legitimate interest in the act for which the account is required?
− How legitimate is that interest?
− Does that interest compete with the legitimate interests of others?
− If there is a conflict created for the person or group required to provide an account, whose interests are more legitimate?

What is to be accounted for?

In an educational system, what is to be accounted for most fundamentally is the welfare of individual students. And within the range of possible meanings of "welfare," most agree on the pre-eminence of academic achievement (Mohrman, Mohrman & Odden, 1996). Such achievement is a necessary if not sufficient part of the meaning of student welfare in the context of schooling.

In current policy and practice, educators are often held accountable, as well, for features of the organization and the practices of those within it believed to contribute more or less directly to students' welfare. One prominent example is characteristics of the school organization identified by research as accounting for variation in its effectiveness (e. g., collaborative professional cultures, high expectations for student achievement, clear goals): these organizational characteristics figure among the criteria government inspectors use in evaluating schools in Scotland and the UK. Another example of what is to be accounted for, other than student welfare directly, are standards of professional teaching practice. In the US context, such standards for advanced teaching have been developed by several agencies, among them the National Board for Professional Teaching Standards (1998). Parallel standards for beginning teaching have been developed by the Interstate New Teacher Assessment and Support Consortium (1992). The Center for Research on Educational Accountability and Teacher Evaluation has developed a taxonomy of teaching "duties" (Scriven, 1994), something else for which educators may be held accountable.

As these illustrations begin to suggest then, in addition to being held accountable for student welfare directly, educators in some contexts are held accountable for:
– ensuring that specific organizational qualities considered to be critical to effectiveness are reflected in their schools or districts;
– organizational efficiency;
– meeting standards of professional knowledge and skill;
– meeting standards of moral behavior;
– performance of best professional practices or specified duties;
– skillfully using organizational processes believed to contribute to the successful introduction of change (such as strategic planning, school improvement planning and the carrying out of quality reviews).

To be comprehensive, then, descriptions and comparisons of different accountability policies and practices need to indicate which of these or other objects of accountability are relevant.

What are the consequences of providing an account?

Providing an account may trigger three responses on the part of the receiving person or group. The first and least consequential of these responses occurs when accounting is voluntary. This would be the case when a teacher voluntarily sends out a newsletter to parents describing what their students program will be like in the next month. In a case such as this, the voluntary nature of the account reduces the likelihood of any response at all that could have connotations of accountability.

A second type of consequence is most likely to occur when an account is obligatory but no consequences have been formally specified. In such cases it seems likely that some response will occur but this response often will be muted and almost by definition will be unpredictable. The requirement, in the Canadian province of Alberta, that school districts annually publish district profiles is an example of an obligatory account unlikely to provoke a predictable response because the form of the response is unspecified. In this case the obligation is a legal one, an obligation spelled out in policy.

But an account also may be considered obligatory on moral grounds. That is, the person or group providing the account may feel that the actions for which they are responsible carry with them an obligation to account by virtue of the special nature of the responsibility. It might well be the case, for example, that the teacher's newsletter is stimulated by a sense of moral obligation the teacher feels to report to parents about the upcoming experiences of the students which their parents have entrusted to her care.

Finally, there are circumstances where an account is required, and rewards and punishments for the person(s) providing the account are specified. Circumstances such as this prevail in some US states (e.g., Kentucky) which require the collection of school-level student performance data. In these states, schools have achievement targets which must be met (Rothman, 1997). When these targets are missed, the school may be placed under review, principals and teachers may be required to implement specific improvement measures, and/or they may be reassigned to other schools.

Wagner (1987) argues that in cases where there is no requirement or obligation that an account be given there is no accountability. But even when only very simple types of reports are expected (descriptions), if there is a requirement or obligation, then this becomes accountability. So some form of obligation or requirement is an essential part of accountability from this perspective. This position rules out, as a form of accountability, the teacher's non-obligatory monthly newsletter, but includes the provincially required district profile even though both are only descriptive in form.

Given this orientation to the consequences associated with giving an account, questions useful for describing and comparing accountability policies and practices should include:

- Is the person obligated or required to provide an account?
- Is the obligation moral and/or legal in nature?
- Are there consequences in the form of rewards or punishments associated with the account?

Alternative approaches to accountability

Accountability has been conceptualized, to this point, in response to five issues: who is accountable, to whom, for what, at what level, and with what consequences. With respect to each of these issues, a set of questions has been identified that could serve as a framework for critically analyzing accountability policies and procedures. Application of such questions, however, is beyond the scope of the present paper (although it would be a productive focus for a subsequent stage of work).

This section of the paper is devoted to a logically prior task, the description and comparison of fundamentally different approaches to accountability. Four such approaches are described, and examples of accountability tools associated with each are identified.

Market competition approaches

This approach to accountability, increasing the competition for students faced by schools, is especially prominent currently, versions of it evident in several European countries, Canada, the United States, New Zealand, Australia and parts of Asia, for example. Specific tools for increasing competition among schools for student-clients include allowing school choice by opening boundaries within and across school systems, school privatization plans, the creation of charter schools, magnet schools, academies and other specialized educational facilities. Competition also is increased by altering the basis for school funding so that money follows students (e.g., vouchers, tuition tax credits), and by publicly ranking schools based on aggregated student achievement scores. These tools are often used in combination.

The common thread binding together these different tools for increasing competition "is a deep disillusionment with the unresponsive and bureaucratic public school monopoly" (Lee, p. 133). Monopolistic, bureaucratic, school systems are believed, by advocates of this approach, to have little need to be responsive to pressure from their clients because they are not likely to lose them. Without natural market forces pressing for and shaping product-client exchanges, the organization tends to develop "product and production orientations" (Hanson, 1992). In relation to schools, this means that they will come to view their major task as offering programs that *they* believe are good for their clients: such organizations seek efficiency on their own terms and are prone to view clients as objects to be treated rather than customers to be served.

The goal of this approach to accountability, then, is to transform schools from "domestic" to "wild" organizations, to use Carlson's (1965) terms; from organizations that do not have to "forage for their fodder," receiving almost all of their funding through average daily attendance of students, to organizations that must struggle and compete for resources to survive. A wild organization, one with a customer orientation, aims to service the needs and wants of target markets through communication, product design, proper pricing, and the timely delivery of services (Kotler & Andreasen, 1987).

In reference to school choice, in particular, advocates of this approach to educational accountability (e.g., Chubb & Moe, 1990) hold a series of assumptions about how such competition is likely to result in greater student achievement. First, increased competition allows parents and students to select schools with which they are more satisfied and which better meet their educational needs. Second, parents who are more satisfied with their child's school provide greater support to that school and to their child's learning. Third, students are likely to be more engaged when their own learning styles are matched to a particular school. Fourth, when teachers have chosen their work settings and have been active in designing their own schools' programs, they will be more committed to implementing those programs effectively. Finally, all of these outcomes will combine to increase student achievement, attendance, and educational attainment (Elmore, 1987; Raywid, 1992).

How does this approach to accountability address the five issues framing the conception of accountability in this paper? In terms of the level of accountability to be provided, market approaches clearly require accounts to offer not only description and explanation but justification, as well. For the most part, it is the direct deliverer of service who is held to account, and the immediate receiver of the service to whom the account is most directly owed, although others such as governments or local districts may also demand an account. "Customer satisfaction" is what is owed. While the information required for such satisfaction may take forms similar to the information required by other approaches to accountability, the central point is that the customer determines what that information should be. And, finally, the consequences of failing to provide an account considered satisfactory by the customer may be fatal to the survival of the school organization under some manifestations of this approach to accountability.

Decentralization of decision-making approaches

Underlying most of the tools for increasing schools' competition for students is the assumption that clients' power to shape the educational services they receive depends on their ability to choose those services which they prefer. This is one of two options Hirschman (1970) argued are available for improving the services of monopolies, an option he referred to as "exit." His other option was "voice;" remaining with the school to which your children are assigned, even though you may be dissatisfied with it, and working toward its improvement.

When decentralization or devolution of decision-making is used for purposes of increasing accountability, one of its central aims often is to increase the voice of those who are not heard (or at least not sufficiently listened to) in the context of typical school governance structures. When this is the goal, a *community-control* form of site-based management (e. g., Bryk et al., 1993; Malen, Ogawa & Krantz, 1990; Wohlstetter & Mohrman, 1993) typically is the instrument used for its achievement. The basic assumption giving rise to this form of site-based management is that the curriculum of the school ought to directly reflect the values and preferences of parents and the local community (Ornstein, 1983; Wohlstetter & Odden, 1992). School professionals, it is claimed, typically are not as responsive to such local values and preferences as they ought to be. Their responsiveness is greatly increased, however, when the power to make decisions about curriculum, budget, and personnel is in the hands of the parent/community constituents of the school. School councils in which parent/community constituents have a majority of the membership are the primary vehicle through which to exercise such power.

In the context of community-control site-based management, the responsibility for providing an account is shared between professionals within the school and representatives of the parent, parent and wider community constituency that the account primarily is owed. What is to be accounted for is the range of decisions allocated to the school council (budget decisions, personnel decisions, and the like). The level of accountability is likely to be justification, and the consequences are potentially varied: dissatisfaction with the account could lead to the replacement of the elected parent-members of council. In contexts where councils have extensive decision-making powers (Chicago, for example), newly elected members might replace the school administration and substantially alter decisions made by previous council members.

Devolution of decision-making, however, is sometimes rooted in a broader reform strategy for public institutions generally which Peters has referred to as "new managerialism." According to Peters, new managerialism "... emphasizes decentralization, deregulation and delegation" (1992, p. 269). While there are variants on this approach to accountability among countries, Hood suggests that they share in common a shift in emphasis (a) from policy formulation to management and institutional design; (b) from process to output controls; (c) from

24

organizational integration to differentiation, and; (d) from "statism to subsidiarity" (cited in Peters, 1992).

In countries such as New Zealand and Australia where school reform has been substantially influenced by the philosophy of new managerialism, creating more efficient and cost-effective school administrative structures is a second central goal for devolution. Typically, this goal is pursued through the implementation of an *administrative-control* form of site-based management which increases school-site administrators' accountability to the central, district, or board office for the efficient expenditure of resources. These efficiencies are to be realized by giving local school administrators authority over such key decision areas as budget, physical plant, personnel and curriculum. Advocates of this form of site-based management reason that such authority, in combination with the incentive to make the best use of resources, ought to get more of the resources of the school into the direct service of students. To assist in accomplishing that objective, the principal, may consult informally with teachers, parents, students or community representatives. Site councils are typically established to advise the principal, with membership at the discretion of the principal.

The school administrator is clearly who is accountable with administrative-control approaches to site-based management, the account being owed to the central administration of the school board or district. Achieving or surpassing agreed-upon goals within allocated budgets, along with community satisfaction, are what is to be accounted for typically. This can often be done with descriptive levels of accounting.

Professional approaches

There are two radically different accountability strategies that have a professional orientation. One of these approaches manifests itself most obviously in the implementation of professional-control models of site-based management. The other approach encompasses the standards movement as it applies to the practices of teachers and administrators. What both strategies hold in common is a belief in the central contribution of professional practice in schools to their outcomes. The strategies differ most obviously on which practices they chose for their direct focus: in the case of professional-control site-based management, the focus is on school-level decision-making whereas teachers' classroom instructional and curricular practices are the focus of the standards movement.

Professional-control site-based management increases the power of teachers in school decision-making while also holding teachers more directly accountable for the school's effects on students. The goal of this form of site-based management is to make better use of teachers' knowledge in such key decision areas as budget, curriculum, and occasionally personnel. Basic to this form of site-based management is the assumption that professionals closest to the student have the most relevant knowledge for making such decisions (Hess, 1991), and that full participation in the decision-making process will increase their commitment to implementing whatever decisions are made. Participatory democracy, allowing employees greater decision-making power, is also presumed to lead to greater efficiency, effectiveness and better outcomes (Clune & White, 1988; David, 1989; Mojkowski & Fleming, 1988). Site councils associated with this form of SBM typically have decision-making power and, while many groups (e.g., parents, students, administration) are often represented, teachers have the largest proportion of members.

In relation to our conception of accountability, this approach to accountability holds teachers, as a group, accountable to parents, students and the district office for the overall effectiveness and efficiency of the school. Such accountability is likely to be at the level of justification but the consequences are not clear. Coupled with a choice system, the consequences could include the survival of the school. Without such a context, parental and district oversight, pressure and the like seem the most likely consequences.

Traditional approaches to accountability in the professions emphasizes heavy control of entry to the profession by government, with responsibility for subsequent monitoring of accountability turned over to members of the profession itself (e.g., colleges of physicians, lawyers' bar associations). Such an approach requires clear standards of professional knowledge, skill, and performance, something the professional standards movement in education set out to define beginning in the US, for example, in the early 1980s. Different products of the standards movement in education are available by now as the basis for the licensure of entry-level teachers (e. g., INTASC's Model Standards for Beginning Teacher Licensing, Assessment and Development) and school administrators (e. g., State of Connecticut Department of Education) as well as for recognizing advanced levels of teaching (e. g., The National Policy Board for Teaching Standards), and school administrator performance (e. g., Education Queensland's Standards Framework for Leaders).

By themselves, standards hold the individual professional accountable to his or her client for delivering services that meet or exceed what is specified by the standards. As part of a licensure system, the professional is held accountable to the government, and beyond the license, one's professional association of colleagues. Standards require professionals to justify failure to practice in ways consistent with the standards. In the context of licensure and post-entry professional associations, failure to comply with standards carries the potential of being barred from entry to the profession, being censured, being limited in one's professional activities, and being removed from the profession.

As this discussion indicates, neither professional teaching or administrator standards by themselves constitute a complete accountability system. Urbanski (1998) has proposed a more comprehensive professional system of accountability which includes, but extends considerably beyond, the use of such standards. He argues that a professional accountability system will include means for ensuring practices that are knowledge-based and client-oriented. It will do this by creating policies, practices, safeguards, and incentives that (a) encourage commitments to the welfare of students, first of all (b) ensure that all individuals practice capabilities in which they are competent (c) require that knowledge be the basis for practice where it exists, and where the knowledge base is uncertain, that (d) practitioners will continually seek to discover the best courses of action.

Applied to schools, this professional model of accountability specifies what teachers, the school and its governance structures, and the district should be accountable for. Teachers, Urbanski (1998) claims, should be accountable for:

"... identifying and meeting the needs of individual students responsibly and knowledgeably, based on standards of professional practice: for continually evaluating – using assessment information and many different feedback sources from parents, students, and their colleagues – how well their practices are accomplishing this goal; for seeking new knowledge and information; and for continually revising their strategies to better meet the needs of students" (p. 456).

The school and its governing structures should be accountable for:

"... equity in the internal distribution of resources; for adopting policies that reflect professional knowledge; for establishing organizational configurations that support teaching and learning; for creating problem-identification and problem solving processes that continually assess and modify its own practices; and for responding to parent, student, and staff concerns and ideas" (p. 456).

And the central office must be accountable for:

"... evaluating the utility and effects of all of the policies that it adopts, such as hiring policies and paperwork requirements; and for equity in the distribution of school resources, including qualified and highly experienced staff and rich curriculum opportunities. It should also be accountable for creating processes that make the school district responsive to the needs and concerns of parents, students, and the school-level staff" (p. 456).

Management approach

Not to be confused with "new managerialism," this approach includes systematic efforts to create more goal-oriented, efficient and effective schools by introducing more rational procedures. The main assumption

28

underlying this approach is that there is nothing fundamentally wrong with current school structures. Nevertheless, their effectiveness and efficiency are improved to the extent that they become more strategic in their choices of goals, and more planful and data-driven about the means used to accomplish those goals. This approach encompasses a variety of procedures for "strategic planning," especially at the district-level, as well as multiple procedures for school improvement planning (see the states of Illinois, Florida and Missouri, for example), school development planning (Giles, 1997), and monitoring progress (e.g., the accountability reviews carried out by New Zealand's Education Review Office).

When this approach is used, typically it is the organization as a whole that is held accountable but with more responsibility for such accountability on the shoulders of the senior administrator – the principal of the school, for example. The school and its senior administrator are most directly accountable to the next level in the organizational hierarchy, such as the district office supervisor to whom the principal reports. Justification is likely the level of accountability required with the effectiveness of the school in reaching specified goals as what the school is being held accountable for. The consequences of a management approach to accountability are well-established and include such responses as promotions, demotions, managerial interventions, and employee transfers. In non-school organizations, financial incentives and rewards are common (Heneman & Ledford, 1998). These have been attempted in education but without much long-term success (Conley & Odden, 1997).

Summary

This section of the report has accomplished three goals. First, it has provided some background to help understand the timing and reasons for the substantial initiatives undertaken worldwide to increase educational accountability. As we have noted, calls for such an increase began in many countries in the mid 1960s and gained considerable momentum during the mid to late 1980s. Although the timing of such calls for greater educational accountability was common to many countries, the reasons giving rise to these calls were rooted in the particular economic, political and social contexts of those countries. These roots potentially are the source of considerable variation in approaches to accountability. But because many countries share a New Right political context, this variation is more muted than would otherwise be expected.

A second goal in this section of the report was to clarify the meaning of accountability. This was accomplished through a liberal adaptation of Walker's (1989) philosophical analysis of accountability relationships and their moral adequacy. From this analysis, we proposed that accountability approaches, strategies, and tools could be distinguished by the nature of their response to five issues: who is to be held accountable, to whom the account is owed, what is to be accounted for, the level of accountability called for, and the consequences of providing the account.

Finally, four major approaches to accountability were described. These include market-oriented approaches, decentralization of decision-making approaches, professionalization approaches, and managerial approaches. Each of these approaches is built on a unique set of basic beliefs and assumptions about schools and how they can be changed, and each draws on a unique set of accountability tools.

Section B: The Accountability Toolbox

Introduction

The main features of a large sample of the policies, procedures, and instruments presently being used to increase the accountability of schools are summarized in this paper. Subsequently referred to as "tools," each of these policies, procedures, and/or instruments is associated with one of four broad approaches to accountability including a market approach, a decentralization approach, a professional approach, and a managerial approach. Unique sets of beliefs and assumptions about the nature of schools and how they might be improved distinguish the four approaches.

Since this paper describes the range of tools presently in use for increasing school accountability, it is critical at the outset to be clear about the meaning of the term itself. A standard, non-technical definition (based on Webster's 7th New Collegiate Dictionary) suggests that being accountable means being subject to giving an account, being answerable, and capable of being accounted for. The term "account" means giving a report on, furnishing a justifying analysis or explanation, providing a statement of explanation of one's conduct, offering a statement or exposition of reasons, causes, grounds, or motives, or simply providing a statement of facts or events.

Given this generic meaning of accountability, the four basic approaches to accountability, and their associated tools differ in terms of their answers to five questions:

- Who is accountable?
- For what?
- To whom?
- At what level?
- With what consequences?

Subsequent sections of this report are organized around the four broad approaches to accountability. The beliefs and assumptions characteristic of each approach are described, followed by a description of each of the accountability tools associated with the approach.

Tools used for increasing accountability using a market competition approach

This approach to accountability by increasing the competition for students faced by schools, is especially prominent currently. Variations on this approach can be found in the UK, Canada, the United States, New Zealand, Australia and parts of Asia, for example. The common thread binding together these different tools for increasing competition "is a deep disillusionment with the unresponsive and bureaucratic public school monopoly" (Lee, p. 133).

Monopolistic, bureaucratic, school systems are believed, by advocates of this approach, to have little need to be responsive to pressure from their clients because they are not likely to lose them. Without natural market forces pressing for and shaping product-client exchanges, the organization tends to develop "product and production orientations" (Hanson, 1992). In relation to schools, this means that they will come to view their major task as offering programs that they believe are good for their clients. Such organizations seek efficiency on their own terms and are prone to view clients as objects to be treated rather than customers to be served.

The goal of this approach to accountability, then, is to transform schools from "domestic" to "wild" organizations, to use Carlson's (1965) terms; from organizations that do not have to "forage for their fodder," receiving almost all of their funding through average daily attendance of students, to organizations that must struggle and compete for resources to survive. A wild organization, one with a customer orientation, aims to service the needs and wants of target markets through communication, product design, proper pricing, and the timely delivery of services (Kotler & Andreasen, 1987).

In reference to school choice, in particular, advocates of this approach to educational accountability (e. g., Chubb & Moe, 1990) hold a series of assumptions about how such competition is likely to result in greater student achievement. First, increased competition allows parents and students to select schools with which they are more satisfied and which better meet their educational needs. Second, parents who are more satisfied with their child's school provide greater support to that school and to their child's learning. Third, students are likely to be more engaged when their own learning styles are matched to a particular school. Fourth, when teachers have chosen their work settings and have been active in designing their own schools' programs, they will be more committed to implementing those programs effectively. Finally, all of these outcomes will combine to increase student achievement, attendance, and educational attainment (Elmore, 1987; Raywid, 1992).

How does this approach to accountability address the five issues framing the conception of accountability developed for this project? In terms of the level of accountability to be provided, market approaches clearly require accounts to offer not only description and explanation but justification, as well. For the most part, it is the direct deliverer of the service who is held to account, and the immediate receiver of the service to whom the account is most directly owed, although others such as governments or local districts may also demand an account. "Customer satisfaction" is what is owed. While the information required for such satisfaction may take forms similar to the information required by other approaches to accountability, the central point is that the customer determines what that information should be. And, finally, the consequences of failing to provide an account considered satisfactory by the customer may be fatal to the survival of the school organization under some manifestations of this approach to accountability. Customers may "exit" in sufficiently large numbers as to make the maintenance of the school no longer viable.

The specific "tools" for increasing competition among schools for student-clients are highly interdependent: typically they are a "set" of tools to be used in combination, rather than "alternatives" tools, of which only one or two might be selected. Furthermore, there is at least a rough order in which these tools must be used. The establishment of school choice policies must occur fairly early. In their least radical form, such policies open the boundaries within a school district, allowing students and parents to select from any school in the district. Modestly more radical is the opening of boundaries among districts.

School privatization policies are yet more radical. These policies encourage the development of clear alternatives to the public schools, usually specialized educational facilities such as charter schools, magnet schools, and academies. For at least some versions of such privatization to occur, it is necessary to alter the basis for school funding so that money follows students (e. g., vouchers, tuition tax credits).

Within districts with open boundaries, market forces are also introduced by publicly ranking schools based on aggregated student achievement scores.

School choice

A substantial quantity of the literature on school choice is based on the US experience. During the 1983–93 period in the US, school choice became "a cornerstone of federal educational policy. From the ashes of an earlier movement to 'privatize' education through vouchers or tuition tax credits, the current movement has attempted to broaden support for public education" (Lee, 1993).

According to Archibald (1996, p. 90), school choice in the US context:

"... diversifies schools, alters or abolishes attendance areas, introduces more complex registration and admissions policies, changes feeder and transportation patterns, and creates unique information dissemination needs. School choice also changes relationships among schools and also between parents and schools in ways intended to foster competition among schools and consumer power among parents."

There are different theories and approaches to school choice ranging from relatively regulated, public school-only to more laissez-faire privatization models. According to Archibald (1996), however, they all have three features in common: parents (or families) are viewed as consumers of a service (education) and schools are viewed as producers; choice is viewed as introducing market dynamics (e.g., competition, diverse educational options, entrepreneurial action among schools) into school systems; and choice, namely, the market processes it creates, is viewed by proponents as producing benefits superior to those produced without a market – that is, residence based assignment to relatively undiversified schools.

Croninger and Lee (1995) note two competing metaphors for school choice – the marketplace and democracy. These metaphors view school reform processes as either outer-directed (the market orientation) or inner directed (democracy). Choice plans that are intended to be part of increasing accountability are the outer-directed, market driven plans. Outer-directed reforms focus on the form of education. In the case of school choice, this focus is the governance and control of schools. Supporters of such reforms reason that the content will take care of itself, because "people are 'utility maximizers' who should make rational choices that will promote good schools" (Croninger & Lee, 1995, p. 317).

In spite of the amount of recent literature based on the US experience, school choice has been part of educational policy in many other countries for many years. Dronkers (1995), in his examination of choice in the Netherlands, points out that, unlike the US, parents have been able to choose among three publicly funded school systems since the 1920s. These systems include Catholic, Protestant and a religiously neutral private-sector system, with no central board for each, although the Protestant and Catholic schools have coordination bodies nationally that function as lobbies without replacing the mainly local, autonomous boards. Within this system, schools with a higher proportion of disadvantaged students receive more funding than schools with more academically privileged students (Ritzen, et al., 1997).

Results of the Netherland system of school choice, according to Dronkers (1995), have not been as often feared in the US. For example, there has not been created a hierarchy of schools, resources are distribute equally, and no "creaming" of the most able students because of financial possibilities or by geographical constraints on parental choice. Indeed, Dronkers argues that: "The deliberate educational choice of parents and teachers of a specific school will increase the chances that this school will become an educational community in which pupils will perform better" (1995, p. 233).

Privatization

Private schools have been a significant feature of most national school systems for many year. Much of the available evidence suggests that, typically, such schools outperform public schools (Madsen, 1996) but for reasons that are largely unrelated to their private nature (Witte, 1992). A more recent initiative to bring market forces to bear on public schools by governments in the interests of increasing their accountability, however, is to actively support the privatization of formerly public schools and to continue to provide some form of public funding for them. As Rehfuss (1995) explains, privatization aims to substantially reduce the scope and breadth of services provided by government, and to have some version of those services offered by private providers. Such privatization is expected to increase the variety of choices available to parents and students.

Privatization takes several forms. One form centers on funding systems that allow tax dollars to flow to schools of choice directly or through families in the form of tuition tax credits, vouchers, or student-driven, direct school funding (Witte, 1992). Other forms include the development of alternative schools with specialized missions – charter and magnet schools for example – and contracting out the management of schools and school districts (Madsen, 1996).

Schools with specialized missions

Simply opening school boundaries within or across school districts provides parents and students with choice but does not necessarily extend the variation of programs and other qualities of existing schools. Creating publicly funded schools with specialized missions explicitly aims to solve this problem: charter schools and magnet schools are examples of this initiative.

Charter schools. A combination of school restructuring efforts and school choice, charter schools in the US are state supported, therefore public. As Nathan (1996) explains, "the charter concept appeals to people who believe in public education but who want it to be more dynamic and more accountable for results" (1996, p. 20). But typically they are independent of existing public schools, governed by their own boards, and usually autonomous from the traditional school board. They are founded and run by teachers, parents, community groups, and private firms (Premack, 1996). The essential case for charter schools has been outlined by Paris as follows:

> "Those closest to the action know what works. Freeing principals and teachers to develop new practices within their schools will lead to real change. Parental choice can increase competitive pressures on schools to perform or lose students. Giving teachers voice and/or parents an exit, it is argued, can only make things better. Professional discretion and market pressure are more likely to improve schools than national or even central office edicts" (1998, p. 387).

Since 1991, at least half of the US states have passed laws permitting the establishment of charter schools. These schools are free of many regulations faced by regular public schools but are held accountable by their charter, which outlines the terms of their existence and the means through which they will be evaluated. Advocates claim that such schools offer a combination that produces market-style choice among schools and allows and encourages experiments in restructuring. Many charter schools are created in order to pursue their own special view of education, thus Charter schools often have distinctive identities.

While the US charter school movement has resulted in as many as 800 schools in 29 US states (Nathan, 1998), the country-wide decentralization movement in New Zealand has resulted in the requirement that every public school develop its own charter.

Magnet schools. Also a feature of the US school system, magnet schools initially sprang up in response to the challenges of school desegregation legislation. Magnet schools, explain Yu and Taylor (1997), are public schools that offer specialized subject themes or educational methodologies as a way of creating desegregated student bodies. More recently they have also been viewed as means for school improvement, a way to offer an alternative to students who would attend inferior-performing inner city schools (Hausman, et al., 1997).

Magnet schools serve accountability purposes because these different schools present parents with choices, thus increasing competition for students. Public magnet schools, however, do not threaten the survival of other public schools because for the most part the money does not follow the student as directly as is the case with charter schools or individual public schools in the UK.

Some evidence (e. g., Gamoran, 1997) suggests that magnet schools are more effective than regular schools at raising proficiency in science, reading and social studies. Based on such evidence, Gamoran argues that:

"These results are more encouraging for advocates of specialized public schools and public school-choice programs. Magnet schools are more likely to serve disadvantaged students than comprehensive schools, yet they rate at least as well in academic climate, social attachment, and course taking" (1997, p. 14).

Public ranking of schools using aggregated student achievement scores

Increasing competition for students by opening boundaries within districts was described (above) as the most conservative strategy for bringing market forces to bear on schools, for purposes of increasing their accountability. Competitive pressures within his strategy, however, are significantly increased by regularly reporting student achievement results for schools within a district aggregated to the school level. Using government-designed and administered achievement measures, this is a common practice, for example, in the UK, the Canadian province of Ontario (most other provinces as well), and many US states (e. g., Louisiana, Florida, California).

Cross school comparisons of this sort, provided in "league tables" in the absence of any other information, can be quite deceiving, of course. Schools do not play on a level field with respect to the characteristics of their students and other variables influencing student learning. This difficulty with a norm-referenced set of comparison is reduced (but only slightly) by the relatively new practice of individual school target-setting. About the plans for such target-setting in the US state of Louisiana, we are told that:

> "Growth targets represent the progress a school must make every two years to reach the Ten Year Goal. School Performance Scores will first be calculated during Spring 1999 for Grades K-8, and Spring 2001 for Grades 9–12. At the end of the first two years, a new School Performance Score will be calculated for each school, and a new Growth Target will be set for the next two-year interval" (Recommendations For Louisiana's Public Education Accountability System, 1998, p. 2).

Tools used for increasing accountability using a "decentralized decision making" approach

Underlying most of the tools for increasing schools' competition for students is the assumption that clients' power to shape the educational services they receive depends on their ability to chose those services which they prefer. This is one of two options Hirschman (1970) argued are available for improving the services of monopolies, an option he referred to as "exit." His other option was "voice"; remaining with the school to which your children are assigned, even though you may be dissatisfied with it, and working toward its improvement. When decentralization or devolution of decision-making is used for purposes of increasing accountability, one of its central aims often is to increase the voice of those who are not heard (or at least not sufficiently listened to) in the context of typical school governance structures. When this is the goal, a community-control form of site-based management (e.g., Bryk et al., 1993; Malen, Ogawa & Krantz, 1990; Wohlstetter & Mohrman, 1993) typically is the instrument used for its achievement.

Devolution of decision-making, however, is sometimes rooted in a broader reform strategy for public institutions, generally, which Peters has referred to as "new managerialism." According to Peters, new managerialism "... emphasizes decentralization, deregulation and delegation" (1992, p. 269). While there are variants on this approach to accountability among countries, Hood suggests that they share in common a shift in emphasis (a) from policy formulation to management and institutional design; (b) from process to output controls; (c) from organizational integration to differentiation, and; (d) from "statism to subsidiarity" (cited in Peters, 1992).

In countries such as New Zealand and Australia where school reform has been substantially influenced by the philosophy of new managerialism, creating more efficient and cost-effective school administrative structures is a second central goal for devolution. Typically, this goal is pursued through the implementation of an administrative-control form of site-based management.

Community control school-based management

The basic assumption giving rise to this form of site-based management is that the curriculum of the school ought to directly reflect the values and preferences of parents and the local community (Ornstein, 1983; Wohlstetter & Odden, 1992). School professionals, it is claimed, typically are not as responsive to such local values and preferences as they ought to be. Their responsiveness is greatly increased, however, when the power to make decisions about curriculum, budget, and personnel is in the hands of the parent/community constituents of the school.

School councils in which parent/community constituents have a majority of the membership are the primary vehicle through which to exercise such power.

In the context of community-control site-base management, the responsibility for providing an account is shared between professionals within the school and representatives of the parent, parent and wider community constituency that the account primarily is owed. What is to be accounted for is the range of decisions allocated to the school council (budget decisions, personnel decisions, and the like). The level of accountability is likely to be justification, and the consequences are potentially varied: dissatisfaction with the account could lead to the replacement of the elected parent-members of council. In contexts where councils have extensive decision-making powers (Chicago, for example), newly elected members might replace the school administration and substantially alter decisions made by previous council members.

Administrative control school-based management

This form of site-based management aims to increase school-site administrators' accountability to the central district or board office for the efficient expenditure of resources. These efficiencies are to be realized by giving local school administrators authority over such key decision areas as budget, physical plant, personnel and curriculum. Advocates of this form of site-based management reason that such authority, in combination with the incentive to make the best use of resources, ought to get more of the resources of the school into the direct service of students. To assist in accomplishing that objective, the principal, may consult informally with teachers, parents, students or community representatives. Site councils are typically established to advise the principal, with membership at the discretion of the principal.

The school administrator is clearly who is accountable with administrative-control approaches to site-based management, the account being owed to the central administration of the school board or district. Achieving or surpassing agreed-upon goals within allocated budgets, along with community satisfaction, are what is to be accounted for typically. This can often be done with descriptive levels of accounting.

School and district profiles

This accountability tool usually takes the form of a report containing a wide range of information about "input," "process" and "output" characteristics of schools or districts. Sometimes likened to a report card for the school (Parents ask about school profiles, 1996), profiles are intended to reflect stakeholder interests. So, for example, school profiles in the Grande Prairie Public School District in the Canadian province of Alberta provides information about student achievement, school climate, instructional quality, and funding (Mestinsek, 1993). In the Springfield Massachusetts public schools, profiles include information about: student attendance; teacher absence, attitudes of parents, students, and teachers; academic achievement; retention percentages; and some information about student activities and plans. These profiles include, as well, a district achievement standard, a value for the school in relation to that standard, and the degree of change that has occurred from one reporting period to the next.

Profiles are often required of districts as well. This is the case for districts in the Canadian province of Alberta, for example. As one district in that province, the Calgary Board of Education's profile (Annual Education Results Report, Calgary Board of Education, 1996–97) illustrates the types of information to be found in such profiles. There is information about the broad directions set out for the district, financial information, the district's goals for students, standards for performance, and evidence about how well they are being achieved. This profile also includes the districts strategic directions and other information such as statistics on graduation rates.

It is the school or district that is being held accountable to its clients and potential clients when profiles are required. In some cases, the organization is accountable simply at the level of describing themselves, the lowest level of accountability. When this is the case, the consequences are difficult to anticipate and are rarely explicit. However, the information in a descriptive profile potentially informs the decisions of clients whether those decisions are of the "exit" or "voice" type. When this accountability tool is not targeted on strategic information, it is unlikely to stimulate school or district improvement efforts. Rather, it seems better suited to simply demonstrating that the organization is open to public scrutiny.

In some cases, however, profiles do contain information strategically related to the school's or district's improvement efforts such as information about needs, goals, and improvement strategies. When this is the case, as in Springfield Public Schools and the Calgary Board of Education, profiles may be aimed at enlisting the support of teachers, parents, and administrators in improving instruction (Howell, 1995).

Tools used for increasing accountability using a "professional" approach

There are two radically different accountability strategies that have a professional orientation. One of these approaches manifests itself most obviously in the implementation of professional control models of school-based management. The other approach encompasses the standards movement as it applies to the practices of teachers and administrators. What both strategies hold in common is a belief in the central contribution of professional practice in schools to their outcomes. The strategies differ most obviously on which practices they chose for their direct focus: in the case of professional control school-based management, the focus is on school-level decision-making whereas teachers' classroom instructional and curricular practices are the focus of the standards movement.

In relation to our conception of accountability, professional control school-based management holds teachers, as a group, accountable to parents, students and the district office for the overall effectiveness and efficiency of the school. Such accountability is likely to be at the level of justification but the consequences are not clear. Coupled with a choice system, the consequences could include the survival of the school. Without such a context, parental and district oversight, pressure and the like seem the most likely consequences.

By themselves, standards hold the individual professional accountable to his or her client for delivering services that meet or exceed what is specified by the standards. As part of a licensure system, the professional is held accountable to the government, and beyond the license, one's professional association of colleagues. Standards require professionals to justify failure to practice in ways consistent with the standards. In the context of licensure and post-entry professional associations, failure to comply with standards carries the potential of being barred from entry to the profession, being censured, being limited in one's professional activities, and being removed from the profession.

Professional control school-based management

Professional-control site-based management increases the power of teachers in school decision-making while also holding teachers more directly accountable for the school's effects on students. The goal of this form of site-based management is to make better use of teachers' knowledge in such key decision areas as budget, curriculum, and occasionally personnel. Basic to this form of site-based management is the assumption that professionals closest to the student have the most relevant knowledge for making such decisions (Hess, 1991), and that full participation in the decision-making process will increase their commitment to implementing whatever decisions are made. Participatory democracy, allowing employees greater decision-making power, is also presumed to lead to greater efficiency, effectiveness and better outcomes (Clune & White, 1988; David, 1989; Mojkowski & Fleming, 1988). Site councils associated with this form of SBM typically have decision-making power and, while many groups (e. g. parents, students, administration) are often represented, teachers have the largest proportion of members.

Professional standard setting

Traditionally, accountability for control of entry into the professions has rested in the hands of government, with responsibility for subsequent monitoring of accountability turned over to members of the profession itself (e.g., colleges of physicians, lawyers' bar associations). This tradition assumes the availability of clear standards of professional knowledge, skill, and performance, something the professional standards movement in education set out to define beginning in the US, for example, in the early 1980s.

Standards for teachers. Many products of the standards movement in education are available by now as the basis for the licensure of entry-level teachers. In the US, considerable credit for stimulating work on the development of teaching standards is attributable to the National Board for Professional Teaching Standards. The Board is: "... an independent, nonprofit, non-partisan organization governed by a 63-member board of directors ..." the majority of whom are classroom teachers. Also included on the board are administrators, school board leaders, politicians, university officials, teacher union leaders and members of the private-sector (About the National Board, 1998).

The Board has developed five major propositions about teaching:
– teachers are committed to students and their learning;
– teachers know the subjects they teach and how to teach those subjects to diverse learners;
– teachers are responsible for managing and monitoring student learning;
– teachers think systematically about their practice and learn from experience;
– teachers are members of learning communities.

On the basis of these propositions, the board is in the process of setting advanced standards for teaching in more than 30 areas. Using these standards as the foundation, the Board has established a two-part process for defining and recognizing highly accomplished teaching. It awards certificates to teachers judged by their peers to meet high standards of practice, that is to "... demonstrate the ability, in a variety of settings, to make sound professional judgements about students' best interests and to act effectively on those judgements" (About the National Board, 1998, p. 1).

Stimulated directly by the National Board's conception of teaching, standards for licensing beginning teachers have been developed by the Interstate New Teacher Assessment and Support Consortium (INTASC). Their Model Standards for Beginning Teacher Licensing, Assessment and Development (1992) propose ten principles of effective beginning teaching and identify the knowledge, dispositions, and performances associated with each. For example, Principle 1 states:

"The teacher understands the central concepts, tools of inquiry, and structures of the discipline(s) he or she teaches and can create learning experiences that make these aspects of subject matter meaningful for students."

Associated with this principle are three knowledge propositions (e.g., "The teacher can relate his/her disciplinary knowledge to other subject areas"), four dispositions (e.g., "The teacher has enthusiasm for the discipline(s) s/he teaches and sees connections to everyday life"), and six performances (e.g., "The teacher can represent and use differing viewpoints, theories, 'ways of knowing' and methods of inquiry in his/her teaching of subject matter concepts").

Examples of other initiatives aimed at identifying standards for teaching can be found in Dwyer (1994), Scriven (1994), and New Zealand's Education Review Office (1998).

Standards for administrators. Standards also have been developed for the licensure of beginning school administrators and for recognizing advanced administrative practice. One well-developed example of such work, intended for both purposes, has been completed for the Connecticut State Department of Education. Starting from a conception of effective school leadership developed for the state (Leithwood & Duke, 1998), these standards consist of 12 broad dimensions of leadership practice, each consisting of associated knowledge and skill, dispositions, and performances. For example, the first broad dimension, concerned with the educated person, states:

"The school leader possesses an understanding of the educated person; and engages staff, parents, and the community in developing a common vision of the educated person and in identifying the implications of that vision for students and the school's programs" (Connecticut State Department of Education, 1996).

Associated with these leadership dimension are four knowledge propositions (e. g., "the school leader understands major historical, and technological developments, and their implications for the knowledge, skills, abilities, and dispositions needed by citizens in today's world"), four dispositions (e. g., "the school leader views cultural diversity as an asset and opportunity"), and five performances (e. g., "the school leader demonstrates sensitivity to and respect for all cultural groups").

The Connecticut work has been extended to include standards for superintendents as well as principals, and to develop assessment tools for judging the extent to which administrators have achieved the standards.

A second, quite recent example of administrator standard is provided by the Australian state of Queensland's Department of Education. The introduction to these standards explains that:

"The Standards Framework for leaders has been developed to form the basis of professional development and training, recruitment and selection of leaders and the credentialling of Education Queensland leaders" (1997, p. 3).

The standards themselves, used to place leaders at one of three levels of credential, are based on six key roles: leadership in education; management; people and partnerships; change; outcomes, and; accountability. With respect to each of these roles, leaders are expected to demonstrate both "best practice competencies," and "personal performance competencies." Best practice competencies are "the knowledge, skills, and behaviors of the leader as exemplified by collective site-based actions of the personnel at the work site" (p. 6). Personal performance competencies are "underlying characteristics of people and indicate behavior across situations and over time" (p. 7). By way of example, a personal performance competency associated with the educational leadership role "leads through vision and values" (p. 7). A best practice competency associated with this same role "operates within an ethical framework" (p. 6).

The document describing Queensland's leader standards also outlines different contexts which should be considered in making judgements about levels of leadership, and the types of evidence that are appropriate to collect about a person's leadership.

Other examples of standards for school leaders include Leithwood and Montgomery (1985), and New Zealand's Education Review Office (1998).

A comprehensive professional accountability model

Neither professional-control school-base management nor teaching and administrator standards by themselves constitute a complete accountability system. Urbanski (1998) has proposed a more comprehensive professional system of accountability which includes, but extends considerably beyond, either of these alternatives. He argues that a professional accountability system will include means for ensuring practices that are knowledge-based and client-oriented. It will do this by creating policies, practices, safeguards, and incentives that (a) encourage commitments to the welfare of students, first of all (b) ensure that all individuals practice capabilities in which they are competent (c) require that knowledge be the basis for practice where it exists, and where the knowledge base is uncertain, that (d) practitioners will continually seek to discover the best courses of action.

Applied to schools, this professional model of accountability specifies what teachers, the school and its governance structures, and the district should be accountable for. Teachers, Urbanski (1998) claims, should be accountable for:

"... identifying and meeting the needs of individual students responsibly and knowledgeably, based on standards of professional practice: for continually evaluating – using assessment information and many different feedback sources from parents, students, and their colleagues – how well their practices are accomplishing this goal; for seeking new knowledge and information; and for continually revising their strategies to better meet the needs of students" (p. 456).

The school and its governing structures should be accountable for:

"... equity in the internal distribution of resources; for adopting policies that reflect professional knowledge; for establishing organizational configurations that support teaching and learning; for creating problem-identification and problem-solving processes that continually assess and modify its own practices; and for responding to parent, student, and staff concerns and ideas" (p. 456).

And the central office must be accountable for:

"... evaluating the utility and effects of all of the policies that it adopts, such as hiring policies and paperwork requirements; and for equity in the distribution of school resources, including qualified and highly experienced staff and rich curriculum opportunities. It should also be accountable for creating processes that make the school district responsive to the needs and concerns of parents, students, and the school-level staff" (p. 456).

Tools used for increasing accountability using a "management" approach

Not to be confused with "new managerialism," this approach includes systematic efforts to create more goal-oriented, efficient and effective schools by introducing systematic management procedures. A fundamental assumption underlying this approach to both accountability and school improvement is that there is nothing fundamentally wrong with current school structures: nevertheless, their effectiveness and efficiency will be improved to the extent that they become more strategic in their choices of goals, and more planful and data-driven about the means used to accomplish those goals. "Cost effectiveness," and "value added" are phrases that capture the mission of those advocating management approaches to accountability, and "control," in its various forms, is the mechanism for accomplishing this mission.

Tools associated with managerial approaches to accountability differ in what it is they aim to control (one or more of the inputs, processes, and outputs of schooling), and how that control is exercised.

Input controls

Many different groups external to the school may be held accountable by this category of controls: governments for policy frameworks and financial inputs; teacher training institutions for preparing competent beginning teachers; community and parents for the value students place on education in general, and schooling in particular, and; the school district for the skills and knowledge of those professionals assigned to the school. These agencies and people are accountable to the public at large, as well as to students, although this relationship is not often acknowledged. What they are being held accountable for is providing the policy, financial, physical, professional and other resources needed by those in the school to accomplish what is expected of the school.

Input controls take a number of specific forms although they are not described in detail in this paper. As one example, the US state of Mississippi developed a set of portfolio and observation-based instruments designed to assess the competence of beginning teachers (Amos, 1992). The competences measured with these instruments included, for example, instructional planning, classroom management, and interpersonal skills. Teacher tests also have been developed in many US states focused on the basic numeracy and literacy skills of teachers (Melnick & Pullin, 1987). Employee recruitment and selection processes (e.g., Pounder & Young, 1996), and financial audits are other examples of specific input controls.

The positive consequences of accountability through the use of input-controls include schools with the capacity to function productively. The failure of such accountability is schools without this capacity. Rarely, however, are there explicit, immediate, negative consequences for those individuals and agencies failing to provide adequate inputs since, typically, they are the most powerful stakeholders in the education system. In the past decade, for example, governments in many countries have reduced the resources available to schools ("getting rid of the fat") and then publicly blamed teachers and administrators for the negative effects of such losses.

In the short run, negative consequences to governments for input failures may take the form of protests to policy, job action (as in Ontario, for example), eroded credibility, and the like, leading in the midterm to a failure to be re-elected. For parents and students the long-term negative consequences are likely to be far-reaching, affecting their social and employment opportunities, for example. For the public-at-large, a less civil and less competitive community may be a consequence.

Examples of tools for increasing accountability through the control of inputs which have been selected for further description here include teacher testing, employee selection processes, and financial auditing.

Process controls

Process controls encompass such tools as program specifications, performance appraisal systems, pay-for-performance schemes, and a variety of planning strategies. For the most part, these tools hold individual school practitioners, or the school's professionals as a group, accountable at the level of justification to those at higher levels of the bureaucracy for the quality of their practices and the goals such practices are intended to accomplish. The consequences of process controls (often in combination with output-controls) are well-established, include employee promotions, demotions, managerial interventions, and employee transfers. In non-school organizations, financial incentives and rewards are common (Heneman & Ledford, 1998). These have been attempted in education but without much long-term success (Conley & Odden, 1997).

Program specifications. Such specifications attempt to clarify at least the ends, goals or outcomes for students that are to serve as the basis for the school's work. Since the early 1970s those concerned with curriculum development and the assessment of student achievement have proposed a variety of approaches for doing this. While setting "standards" for students is the latest of these approaches (e.g., Marsh, 1997; Harris & Carr, 1996), it is not significantly different in form or intent from such earlier approaches as "outcome-based education," setting curriculum aims and objectives, and even specifying "behavioral objectives" (Mager, 1972). One way or another, these approaches are aimed at clarifying the purposes of schooling in more or less detail (their advocates would claim more, of course). Some of these approaches bring a normative perspective to bear on such aims – outcomes-based education is a case in point – others are primarily focused on the importance of clarity itself.

In some circumstances these specifications also outline at least some of the means schools are expected to use in order to help students accomplish such outcomes. For example, many US state curriculum frameworks advocate "constructivist" approaches to instruction. Efforts have been made to specify "opportunity to learn" standards (e.g., Smithson, 1995), specifications of the school and classroom conditions that should be available to students in support of their learning. Program specifications directly address the issue of what it is that schools, and in some cases districts and states, are to be held accountable for.

Performance appraisal systems. Such systems attempt to hold teachers, administrators and other educational workers accountable for their students' achievement, meeting agreed-upon objectives, engaging in role-related practices (e.g., Glassman & Heck, 1996) and/or performing duties considered basic to the job (e.g., Scriven, 1994). Performance appraisal systems typically include a series of steps for arriving at a judgement about performance. Glassman and Heck (1996), for example, outline steps in a role-based assessment such as criteria-setting, delimiting the scope of the evaluation, setting standards, collecting data, making an evaluation decision.

Pay-for-performance schemes. Conley and Odden (1995) distinguish three different approaches to linking teachers to pay schemes. These

alternatives include pay-based on individual or organizational performance, pay-based on the tasks carried out (as in differentiated staffing
plans), and pay-based on knowledge and skills.

Individual performance-based pay, essentially merit pay, has proven
difficult to implement. It produces staff dissension, administrative
problems (such as record keeping, and personnel evaluation), and problems in determining who deserves the extra pay. Many US districts that
implemented such systems have now abandoned them. According to
Conley and Odden (1995), this approach has been abandoned because
educational settings differ from other organizational settings where
merit pay has been more successful. This approach works best "in
settings where the work technology or process is relatively simple and
well understood, straightforward methods can be used to measure performance, and workers and workers efforts are not interdependent"
(1995, p. 220). See also Lawler (1990) and Mohrman et al., (1992).
Individual performance-based plans also assume that extrinsic rewards
offer significant incentives to teachers whereas considerable evidence
suggests that such rewards are by no means the only rewards that motivate teachers.

A second alternative, job-base pay was evident in the career ladder
systems of the 1980s, as well as in earlier differentiated staffing plans
implemented in the late 1960s and early 1970s. Job-based pay, in the
context of career ladders, allocated pay on the basis of the specific
tasks performed by the teacher. Such tasks included taking on additional administrative tasks, etc. The rationale for such an approach was
simply that teacher pay is linked in a fairly objective way to the amount
of work the teacher does, thus avoiding the subjective performance
evaluations that plague merit pay systems. But this approach came
under criticism because of the implication that classroom teaching was
not as important as administrative functions. Further, to be rewarded
within such systems, teachers had to remove themselves from the classroom for at least part of the time.

Examples of locations that implemented job-based pay include Tem-
ple City, California (differentiated staffing in the 1970s) and the State
of Tennessee (career ladder program in the 1990s).

At the present time, skill and knowledge-based pay systems are receiving substantial support. According to Mohrman, Mohrman, & Odden (1996), the components of school reform include a focus on: school performance and student outcomes; new curricula and the professional skills that they require; and a restructuring of the way schools are managed and organized. If this is the case, Mohrman and his colleagues reason, then compensation packages should focus attention on: results by tying them to rewards; the acquisition of the skills needed to implement the new curricula; the knowledge and skill needed to implement new management structures.

As part of this alternative, pay can be tied to indirect assessments of knowledge and skill, as in the traditional practice of paying for years of experience and/or college credits. But pay also can be linked to direct assessments of knowledge and skill, although as yet this has rarely been done in education. Connely and Odden (1995) describe attempts to do so in Flowing Wells, Arizona, Charlotte-Mecklenberg, North Carolina, and Australia. The feasibility of this alternative has been increased considerably by the efforts, reviewed above, to identify explicit teaching standards and procedures for judging the extent to which such standards are being met.

Planning and monitoring. A formal plan typically consists of organizational goals, strategies or actions to be taken for their accomplishment, designated responsibilities for carrying out each strategy, an estimate of the resources needed, and the timelines for implementing the plan. Some plans include, as well, indicators to be used in evaluating the success of the initiatives for which the plan was developed.

A common, process control set of tools for increasing accountability, various forms of planning are advocated to help ensure that short and long-term organizational goals are established in a rational and transparent manner, and that organizational actions are explicitly designed to accomplish such goals. "Strategic planning," "school improvement planning" and "school development planning" are terms which appear in the educational accountability and reform literature signifying different approaches to planning.

Adopted from the corporate sector, school districts or local educational authorities (LEAs), in particular, have devoted considerable energies since the mid-1980s to the development of strategic plans.

54

The US state of Pennsylvania, for example, requires all districts in that state to develop such plans (George, 1993); the UK Department of Education and Science "... in their official guidance for the introduction of [local management of schools] in England and Wales ... envisaged a continuing, albeit temporary, strategic planning role for LEAs" (Giles, 1997, p. 2). In these contexts, the term "strategic" is usually distinguished from the term "operational." Strategic plans are intended to take "the long view" (de Geus). They also are intended to focus on priorities that warrant exceptional organizational attention, either because they represent critical problems that threaten the health of the organization, or because they constitute important new areas for organizational development. In contrast, operational planning focuses on the short term, aiming to ensure that established organizational tasks are carried out efficiently and effectively.

While sharing the same generic planning components outlined above, "school improvement planning" is unique to educational organizations. The source of the label given to this form of planning is the substantial body of research literature identifying factors that influence school improvement (e.g., Fullan, 1992; Louis & Miles, 1992). Strategies or actions included in school improvement plans for accomplishing organizational goals are intended to reflect the results of such research. For example, to accomplish most goals related to improving student learning, a school improvement plan would be expected to reflect the importance of creating a collaborative professional culture in the school (Hargreaves, 1991), applying both pressure and support for teachers to change (Fullan, 1992), and structuring the school to allow adequate opportunities for ongoing professional learning.

In addition to the research on school improvement, some approaches to school improvement planning also reflect the results of research on the characteristics of effective schools. Creating these characteristics becomes the short-term goal of these plans, with improvement in student learning typically the long-term goal. Stoll and Fink (1992) provide a well-tested set of guidelines for developing and monitoring this type of plan.

A number of national and sub-national governments now require some version of school improvement planning from all schools. This is the case, for example, with the US state of Illinois' "quality review" and "improvement planning" process required of all schools in that state (ISBE Accountability & Quality Assurance, 1998). This process orients schools toward three major areas of their organizations: teaching and learning; student learning, progress and achievement; and the learning community. The focus of each of these areas is further specified. With respect to "the learning community," for example, schools are directed to examine their mission and vision, leadership and administration, organizational structure, professional development, and community participation. Other states with comparable requirements include, for example, Louisiana (Recommendations for Louisiana's Public Education Accountability System, 1998), Florida (The Basics of School Improvement and Accountability in Florida, 1997–98), and Missouri (Missouri School Improvement Program, 1998). Appendix – includes sample material from the policies and procedures of these states.

A version of school improvement planning, called "school development planning," is common to virtually all schools in England and Wales having been introduced by the Department of Education and Science in the context of its local management of schools initiative included in the 1988 Education Reform Act (Giles, 1997). The recommended planning process is cyclical, beginning with an audit of the school to identify priorities for attention, followed by construction of the plan, implementation and evaluation leading to a new cycle (Hargreaves et al., 1990; MacGilchrist, et al., 1995; Cuckle et al., 1998). Such planning "... is said to enable priorities for development which incorporate local and national requirements as well as school-generated concerns to be established" (MacGilchrist et al., 1995, p. 9).

Output controls

Both student achievement standards, and various approaches for measuring, reporting, and acting on student achievement are examples of initiatives to increase accountability, through the use of output controls. Such controls may be targeted at the accountability of students and/or

56

those professionals, usually teachers and school administrators, directly responsible for facilitating student achievement. Individual parents, school governors in decentralized systems, and school district officials are those to whom the account is owed. In some jurisdictions this account is owed, as well, to national, state or provincial governments as well, who use the data for planning system-wide improvement initiatives or to dispense various types of rewards for exceeding, or punishments for failing to meet, predetermined achievement targets.

By themselves, student achievement standards, and data resulting from their measurement provide only descriptive levels of accountability. But such output controls are rarely implemented by themselves. In combination with the rewards and punishments mentioned above, for example, the level of accountability called for is justification.

Student standards. The setting of standards for students, widespread in North America (Davis, 1998), may be interpreted as a significant step beyond traditional goal-setting activities that have been a characteristic part of curriculum development, at least in North America, since Ralph Tyler (1949) published his now-classic text. While such goal-setting specified what it was that students were to learn, standards establish the levels or degrees of sophistication of such learning. This is a task that in the past was left to measurement specialists in the context of establishing what responses from students would count as mastery of a given curriculum objective. Unlike the detailed specification of acceptable responses that was the outcome of the work of test developers, however, standards (or benchmarks) typically are quite broad or general.

When conceived of as accountability tools, student standards are assumed to make important contributions to school improvement by setting precise performance targets at which schools can aim. Tracking student progress is aided with such standards. School improvement planning, it is assumed also, can be more strategic with such targets. And when standards are set outside the school, they provide consistency of service across schools in the same jurisdiction.

Such assumptions may not always be warranted, however. In a study carried out in two US districts in the state of Wisconsin, for example, Derlin found that:

"... accountability standards overall create minimal expectations for districts, and accountability reporting had only limited influence on education practices" (1991, abstract).

This was the case even though these districts' policies shifted accountability for student outcomes to the individual school, and the schools were believed to be fully complying with policy.

Student testing. The undisputed "bottom line" for schools is contributing to growth, at minimum, in students' knowledge and skills. Curriculum policies in most jurisdictions typically include goals, outcomes or standards for students in social, emotional, and value domains as well. So it is not surprising that, as an accountability tool, student testing is ubiquitous. In Canada, for example, all provinces engage in some form of province-wide assessment of student achievement.

Furthermore, national comparisons of student achievement are now a regular part of the international educational policy environment in the context of such projects as the Third International Mathematics and Science Study conducted by the International Association of Educational Achievement in 1995 (Earl & Nagy, 1998). The implementation of student testing policies for accountability purposes raises two issues, in particular, that are contentious and complex: How will results be used? and In what form will results be reported?

The most common focus of student tests for accountability purposes is discipline-related basic knowledge and skills. A recent movement toward "authentic" (e. g., Neil) and performance-based tests (e. g., Darling-Hammond, Ancess & Falk, 1995) has expanded this focus to more complex domains and competencies that approximate the requirements of real-life problem solving and a wider range of the goals typically included in curriculum guidelines and frameworks. This is an important development, since it is widely assumed that "what gets tested gets taught." The steering effects of tests on curriculum and instruction are well documented and to the extent that this is true, narrowly conceived tests are likely to "dumb down" the curriculum that actually gets taught.

How the results of student tests are reported is the most important factor in determining the nature of accountability created by such tests.

Consider two common methods of reporting: jurisdiction-wide, and school-by-school reporting. With jurisdiction-wide reporting of results, the national, province, state-wide education authorities and the programs that they sponsor are being held accountable to the public at large. Because such results almost always are compared to "benchmarks" or "standards" for evaluation purposes, the level of accountability typically is justification and the consequences often entail fine-tuning of the jurisdiction's programs. There may be consequences, as well, for the trust and regard awarded school practitioners by politicians and taxpayers. Politicians routinely seize on "sub-standard" results to promote their own platforms, whether or not this is warranted (see Berliner & Biddle, 1996).

With school-by-school reporting of results, in conjunction with school choice, student testing becomes a tool for pursuing market approaches to accountability as discussed above. Without choice, student testing still holds school professionals accountable more directly to parents and district officials. But the consequences are not predictable.

Comprehensive controls

Several accountability tools attempt to be comprehensive in what it is they seek to control. This is the case for school inspections, as well as school and district monitoring systems, and indicator systems.

School inspection. The UK, Scotland and New Zealand are examples of countries with well-developed inspection systems. These systems are labeled "comprehensive" management approaches to accountability because they are able to, and typically do, take into account evidence concerning inputs, processes, and outcomes. Inspections of primary schools uses 33 performance indicators to answer questions concerning how well pupils are performing, how well the school is managed, and how effective is the school.

Key criteria guiding the inspection process include:
- achievement of outputs, particularly student achievement;
- quality of learning and teaching;

- responsiveness to aims, circumstances and key features of the school;
- adequacy of the school's development plan and targets;
- responsiveness to parent views;
- consistent use of performance indicators;
- flexibility within a clear framework of procedures.

Inspection systems such as Scotland's hold the staff of the school to account: staff are being asked to provide not only a description and explanation of their work but justification, as well. It is parents, the school's governing body, the local education authority, and the government to whom schools are accounting through most of this inspectoral process.

Monitoring and indicator systems. These two accountability tools share important features but also differ in important respects. An educational indicator, in Oakes' terms, is "a statistic about the educational system that reveals something about its performance or health" (1986, p. 1). As Darling-Hammond explains:

"Indicators summarize information on variables with policy, political, and theoretical significance. They are 'individual or composite statistics that reflect important features of a system, such as education, health or the economy'" (Darling-Hammond, 1992, cited in Archibald, 1996, p. 4).

Indicators systems may or may not be comprehensive. For example, Educational Indicators in Canada (Canadian Education Statistics Council, 1996) includes indicators of some of the inputs and contexts for Canadian education along with information about outputs (achievement in reading, writing and mathematics, for example). But this indicator system is silent on those educational processes characteristic of Canadian schools and school systems. Indicator systems hold educational systems accountable to the public at large, at the level of description.

In comparison, a monitoring system is a framework within which to select or define, interpret and use a wide array of indicators (Richards, 1998). The central distinction between a system of indicators and a monitoring system is the requirement, in the case of a monitoring system, that regularly collected information be translated into courses of action. These courses of action will usually be informed by the strategic directions established by the educational system. To serve this purpose, then, a monitoring system must be based on a coherent understanding of what is being monitored. And such an understanding is considerably assisted by information not only about inputs and outputs but processes and the relationships among them, as well. By way of example, the monitoring system developed by Leithwood and Aitken (1995), and used in a handful of school systems to date, collects information about each of these sorts of factors and provides assistance in analyzing and interpreting the information collected about them.

Monitoring systems form the basis for accountability at the level of justification, and their consequences are anticipated to be actions by those in the educational system intended to change organizational processes likely to influence the achievement of outputs considered to be in need of strategic attention.

Summary

This section of the report has described a large number of quite specific tools used for the purpose of increasing the accountability of schools, school districts and larger educational jurisdictions such as provinces, states and nations. These tools encompass most of the "reform" and "restructuring" initiatives that have been advocated for education over the past decade, reminding us that accountability has been, undoubtedly, the pre-eminent goal for reformers during this period.

Those accountability tools described in this section emerge from four distinctly different approaches to accountability – a market approach, a decentralization approach, a professionalization approach, and a managerial approach. In the case of each approach and tools associated with it, this section described underlying assumptions as well as at least examples of the specific tools arising from such assumptions.

Market approaches to accountability increase the competition among schools and districts for students. They do this on the assumption that monopolistic organizations are neither efficient nor sensitive to the needs of their clients. Opening school and district boundaries, privatizing schools, and developing schools with specialized missions are among the tools used as part of this approach to accountability. In conjunction with more flexible allocation of funding e.g., vouchers, tuition tax credits, these tools allow parents and students to "exit" schools with which they are dissatisfied and find schools more to their liking. Publicly ranking schools using aggregated student achievement scores, another tool associated with the market approach, provides parents and students information to help inform their choices.

A second approach to accountability is decentralization of decision-making authority and the tools associated with this approach are several forms of site-based management. One of the central aims of decentralization is to increase the voice of those who are not heard (or at least not sufficiently listened to) in the context of typical school governance structures. The assumption in this case is that "exit" is not the only means of giving parents more power in shaping their childrens' school experiences. Another option is to give parents and students more "voice" in improving the school to which children are assigned in a non-choice context. When this is the goal, community-control forms of site-based management are the tools used for its achievement.

Decentralization of decision-making authority, however, is some-times rooted in a broader reform strategy for public institutions, gener-ally, which is referred to as "new managerialism." In countries where school reform has been substantially influenced by new managerialism, the underlying assumption is that public institutions, schools included, are inefficient and not generally cost-effective. Administrative-control forms of site-based management are considered to be effective tools for ameliorating these shortcomings.

There are two radically different accountability strategies that have a professional orientation. One of these approaches manifests itself most obviously in the implementation of professional-control models of school-based management. The other approach encompasses the stand-ards movement as it applies to the practices of teachers and administra-tors. What both strategies hold in common is a belief in the central contribution of professional practice in schools to their outcomes. The strategies differ most obviously on which practices they chose for their direct focus: in the case of professional control school-based management, the focus is on school level decision-making whereas teachers' classroom instructional and curricular practices are the focus of the standards movement.

Not to be confused with "new managerialism," managerial approaches to accountability include systematic efforts to create more goal-oriented, efficient and effective schools by introducing systematic management procedures. A fundamental assumption underlying this approach to accountability is that there is nothing fundamentally wrong with current school structures. Nevertheless, their effectiveness and efficiency will be improved to the extent that they become more strategic in their choices of goals, and more planful and data-driven about the means used to accomplish those goals. "Cost effectiveness," and "value added" are phrases that capture the mission of those advocating management approaches to accountability, and "control," in its various forms, is the mechanism for accomplishing this mission. Tools associated with managerial approaches to accountability differ in what it is they aim to control (one or more of the inputs, processes, and outputs of schooling), and how that control is exercised.

Section C: Accountability Policies and Practices in Selected Countries

Introduction

While the four approaches to accountability discussed in the previous section are conceptually quite distinct, accountability policies and procedures adopted by governments and other authorities tend to be highly eclectic. Such eclecticism is not always bad, of course. The eight parts of this section, summarizing a significant sample of accountability policies and procedures adopted in eight selected countries, illustrate the nature of this eclecticism in practice. The countries include Scotland, The Netherlands, Norway, New Zealand, Canada, Germany, Hungary, and Switzerland.

Information used as the basis for describing accountability policies and procedures came from a variety of sources. Informants in each of the eight countries suggested by Bertelsmann Foundation staff provided relevant documents, as well as their own written overviews of such policy in several cases. Electronic data bases likely to include relevant information were searched, and in the case of most of the eight countries, information contained on official Websites reviewed. Relevant, non-English language documents were analyzed by native language speakers in the case of the Netherlands, Hungary, Germany, Norway, and Switzerland. In spite of these efforts, we do not claim that what is described in this section captures more than a sample of accountability policies and practices in any of the eight countries. The entire project was completed within a four-month period of time precluding follow-up initiatives beyond what is described here that would yield a more comprehensive picture of policies in each country.

Also described in each of the parts making up this section are the perspectives of teachers and school administrators on accountability in their own schools, and on the accountability policies and procedures established by the larger systems within which their schools are located. These are the perspectives of a "convenience sample" of approximately ten teachers and principals from two schools in each of the eight countries: the extent to which their responses represent the views of other teachers and principals in their countries cannot be known. But they do begin to suggest the extent to which the meaning and intents of "official" system policies are subject to "adaptation" at the local level.

Teachers and administrators offered their views on accountability in response to five general questions asked by local data collectors usually in the first language of the respondents. These questions were as follows:

– How do you understand the term "accountability" in the context of your own school and classroom?
– Who are your clients? Who are the other stakeholders? What are some examples of their needs and wants?
– What do you do at the present time that might be considered "accountability" according to your own understanding of that term?
– What initiatives from the [school district or other comparable] level can you identify that seem to be aimed at increasing accountability?
– What initiatives from the [national or other comparable] level can you identify that seem to be aimed at increasing accountability?

For the most part, responses were summarized by the local data collectors and forwarded to the principal investigators, along with tape recordings of the interviews.

Scotland

Background

Public-sector education in Scotland is a partnership between central and local government. The Secretary of State for Scotland is responsible to the United Kingdom Parliament for the overall supervision and development of the education system in Scotland. The Secretary of State exercises his responsibility for education through the Scottish Office of Education, and Industry Department (SOEID). SOEID has national oversight of education, advises on national policy and coordinates the activities of education authorities and others. It also issues guidance on such matters as curricula, teaching and learning, self-evaluation and development planning. The provision and management of education is the responsibility of 32 locally elected councils. These councils, as the local education authorities, have a statutory duty to provide adequate and efficient preschool and school education and to make provision for special education needs. They are responsible for the construction of buildings, the employment of teachers and other staff and the provision of equipment and materials. The education authorities exercise responsibility for the curriculum taught in schools, taking into account national guidance.

Education is compulsory for all children from ages five to 16, although over two-thirds continue with their school education for at least a further year. Schools are organized as primary (seven years beginning at age five) and secondary (generally six years from age 12 to 18).

The partnership in Scottish Education manifests itself in the Quality-Initiative in Scottish Schools. This initiative promotes school self-evaluation, in particular, through the publication of *How good is our school?* which provides a framework for schools to review their own practice. All education authorities have been involved in this initiative, not only in their promotion of self-evaluation and school development planning, but through participation in seminars and involvement in a range of developments promoted by the partnership between education authorities, schools and HM Inspectors of Schools (Scotland).

Accountability policies in Scotland

HMI school inspections

HM Inspectors of Schools (Scotland) has responsibility for national monitoring of the education system. It analyzes and publishes evidence of how well schools, education authorities, and colleges are performing. In primary schools, these inspections take place within a two-week period and involve inspection of all aspects of the work of the school, with particular focus on attainment across the curriculum. In secondary schools a core team inspects whole-school aspects of provision and a larger team, with subject specialists, examines a cross-section of subject departments. Prior to inspection, parents, the education authority and the school board are invited to express their views, and at the end of inspection, head teachers and staff complete an evaluation questionnaire about the process.

The inspection uses 33 performance indicators to answer questions concerning how well pupils are performing, how well the school is managed, and how effective is the school. Key criteria guiding the inspection process include:
- achievement of outputs, particularly student achievement;
- quality of learning and teaching;
- responsiveness to aims, circumstances and key features of the school;
- adequacy of the school's development plan and targets;
- responsiveness to parent views;
- consistent use of performance indicators;
- flexibility within a clear framework of procedures.

The management and staff of the school is most directly being held to account, and they are being asked to provide not only a description and explanation of their work (evidence), but justification, as well. Oral feedback is provided to staff and the head teacher, and a draft report is discussed with them, also. Nonetheless, it is parents, the school board, the local education authority, and the Scottish government to whom schools are accounting through the inspectoral process. A published report is available to teachers, school board, and parents.

The inspectoral report highlights strengths of the school and also contains the main points for action by the school and education authority. These recommendations for actions are expected to be implemented, or at least incorporated into the school development plan, within 12 to 18 months of the publication of the report. Conclusions of follow-up inspections are published in the form of a letter from the chief inspector to the head teacher, education authority and chairperson of the school board, and the letter is available to the same persons who received the original inspection report. If progress is unsatisfactory, a further inspection takes place within a specific time frame.

Inspection findings across multiple schools are used to evaluate the performance of the system as a whole and a national Standards and Quality Report which outlines the quality of education in Scottish Schools as evidenced from the inspection program is published every three years.

School development planning

Each school is required to have a School Development Plan based on a three-year cycle with the first year of the plan described in detail and the remaining two years described in outline form. The plan should reflect school, national and local educational authority priorities. It also must take into account the views of the school board, parents, and staff.

The planning process is intended to include annual reports of progress on previous year's performance against targets. A detailed plan for the subsequent year is then expected, as well. The plan is intended to be a program for implementation within the school with the major focus being related directly to teaching and learning. School development plans are required to include aims, an audit, and statements of actions to be undertaken. The school development plan is seen as an important enabling mechanism by means of which today's changes can be introduced in a planned and sensitive manner, while yesterday's changes are consolidated and improved, and tomorrow's are recognized as having their place.

Aims are broad statements of the school's directions, expressed in terms easily understood by parents, teachers, pupils and the wider community. The audit reports the results of a systematic evaluation of the school's current performance in key areas of its work, related to its aims and available resources. It includes judgments about the quality of education in the school, indicating particular strengths and weaknesses. Both qualitative and quantitative performance indicators, as well as views of parents, pupils, school boards and teachers are to be used in an audit. An audit contains an evaluation of ongoing aspects of the school's work in addition to identifying priorities for development. The audit is described in more detail below.

School development plans also are required to specify the actions to be taken to achieve targets for the coming year. These targets are derived from the aims and the audit. The action section of a school development plan includes targets, criteria for success, implementation strategies, a timescale, resources and evaluation procedures.

School development planning holds the school staff accountable for describing, explaining and justifying its initiatives. The school's educational authority approves its plan. School board members receive a copy of the plan and parents are informed of its availability. School development plans provide HMI with data that could affect the nature of the HMI evaluation during the inspection process. Such plans also contribute to parental awareness of a school's effectiveness.

School self-evaluation

Individual schools are responsible for self-evaluation, but the Audit Unit of HMI took the lead in providing support materials and developing the 33 performance indicators that schools are expected to use. The indicators and the approaches to school self-evaluation are set out in a national publication "How good is our school?: Self-evaluation using performance indicators." School self-evaluation is the basis of the Audit section of a school development plan, but also serves a function beyond that in enabling the school to evaluate the quality of the education it provides for its students. Development planning is seen to be a good way into the self-evaluation process. The school self-evaluation draws on the same performance indicators as used by HMI in an external inspection. School self-evaluation is viewed as being the heart of quality assurance and provides the information to produce the school's report on standards and quality.

The evaluation, to be written by the headteacher, is based on three questions:

- How are we doing? – this questions asks schools how they are performing in relation to their aims for the school/classroom/department. It involves a broad view of performance across seven key areas: curriculum, attainment, learning and teaching, support for students, ethos, resources, management and leadership and quality assurance. Schools then take a closer look at specific areas viewed as successful or causing concern.
- How do we know? – this question asks schools to compare their achievements with expectations described in their aims. The question requires the use of a whole range of data, including school-based student assessments, school ethos indicators that take account of views of pupils, parents and teachers, national reports on attendance or examinations of school costs, standard tables of examination results, and the 33 performance indicators providing comprehensive coverage of the seven key areas.
- What are we going to do now? – this is a question about key strengths and it requires a school to identify levels of service to be maintained. It also asks the school to identify development needs, a manageable numbers of priorities, and to set specific achievable and measurable targets.

The self-evaluation report (Standards and Quality report) is shared with the school community on a three-year cycle (as part of the school development plan process). Annual updates are provided for internal school use, based on the school development plan. Results of the self-evaluation provide an agenda for discussion with officers of the education authority and inform their view of standards and quality across all the schools within the authority.

School self-evaluation becomes the basis for data-driven school improvement decisions, and for communicating with parents and other members of the school community. The report of the evaluation is used for planning appropriate support from education advisory services, and becomes part of the data base for defining the standards and quality of education within the educational authority as well as nationally.

Setting standards for student achievement

In March 1998, the Scottish Office announced a new policy building on inspections, school development planning and school self-evaluation. The government set up an Action Group on Standards to advise on setting student achievement targets for schools, such targets to be set for 2001. Schools are being asked to set their own targets in key areas of attainment and basic skills of literacy and numeracy. Targets are to be based on average attainment over the most recent three years.

The Action Group, after consultation, developed five principles to guide the target-setting process. The targets should be:
– set in a manner consistent across the nation
– limited in number and focused on key priorities
– simple, clear, and quantifiable
– realistic and achievable taking into account current performance and that of other schools with similar characteristics
– set, evaluated and reported on by schools, educational authorities, and SOEID working in partnership.
The HMI Audit Unit will support target setting by providing bench-marking information and other supporting materials. The Audit Unit will also develop a School Characteristics Index to identify schools with similar characteristics. Each school, in consultation with its education authority, will decide the target level of improvement to be incorporated in its development plan.

The target areas are intended to reflect issues of concern identified in HMI's Standard and Quality Reports and other publications. As well, the targets are to be central to the interests of parents and pupils, and consistent with government priorities. Setting targets in priority areas will, it is believed, promote a more focused approach to self-evaluation, ensure best use of existing data, and build on work already in progress. Schools will be held accountable for reaching targets and educational authorities are accountable for assisting schools. The targets themselves, however, are not an end in themselves. They are a focus for planning for improvement. Having set targets, schools will then have to plan how they are to be achieved.

National student achievement testing

The HMI Audit Unit will be collecting achievement data for all schools. As part of the national curricular program for all students aged five to 14 teachers assess students and confirm these assessments in reading, writing, mathematics by means of national tests, but the results are used in the schools to plan programs of study for individual students and are not collected by the Audit Unit.

There are very clear data for secondary schools about student performance and school leaver destination aggregated by school, educational authority, and nationally for easy comparison of individual schools within authorities and across the nation, as a whole. In addition, a bar graph is prepared for each school board which compares the individual school results with average national results. Tables of information on a school's examination results are made available to the head teacher and education authority. These tables enable comparison of student performance among departments within a school.

Parents are the primary audience for the data, reflecting a commitment in The Parents' Charter in Scotland to provide more and better information about quality and standards in schools. Reports are public documents available to anyone who wishes to view them. This allows for a comparison of schools' raw data without full information about school characteristics.

Decentralized decision-making

As of April 1996, all education authorities were to have introduced local schemes of Devolved School Management (DSM): this initiative was introduced without prior legislation. The first phase of DSM began in 1994 although one region introduced its own scheme in 1990. Broad guidelines give each authority flexibility in how they operate their DSM scheme.

The aim of DSM is to ensure that decisions on the day-to-day management of schools are taken at the school level. DSM was not intended to weaken the responsibility of education authorities for providing education services in their area. It was intended, rather, to allow them to focus more on strategic planning and providing support to local schools.

DSM places more responsibility and therefore accountability on head teachers who are powerful advisors to school boards in Scotland. But in moving to more local decision-making, with more involvement by parents, and greater discretion by the head teacher, accountability is being shared by more people in more roles. One clear, potential consequence of DSM is more parent involvement in the local school and possibly greater awareness across the community about the school's activities.

Teaching standards

Teachers working in Scottish state schools must be registered with the General Teaching Council (GTC). At present there is no formal statement of standards to be achieved at the end of the two-year probationary period. The GTC has been asked to develop standards teachers must meet to be granted full registration after their probation.

A July 7, 1998 news release issued by the Minister of Education indicated that he had just issued a consultation document on the development of a framework for the continuing professional development of the teaching profession. The consultation process was to end on October 10, 1998. The consultation paper contained a framework of competencies, standards, and associated qualifications covering the wide range of tasks teachers undertake at different stages of their careers. Elements of the proposed framework are:
- a statement of the teaching standards probationer teachers must reach in order to be granted full registration by the GTC;
- guidance on how continuing professional development might be developed and given more focus;

- career development for classroom teachers;
- career development for new roles, possibly leading to advanced professional qualifications for teachers with senior management and other responsibilities.

Draft guidelines also have been developed for Initial Teacher Education courses. Reaction to the documents were to be submitted by May 29, 1998. In addition to listing the degree requirements for primary and secondary teachers, the guidelines proposed a list of about 50 competencies student teachers would be expected to acquire. The competencies encompass knowledge, understanding, critical thinking, and practical skills. The competencies listed were related to:

- subject and content of teaching;
- classroom communication and approaches to teaching and learning, class organization and management, and assessment;
- broader aspects of the school;
- the values, attributes and abilities integral to professionalism.

School-level perspectives on accountability in Scotland

This section describes the results of interviews with a small number of staff members, from a "convenience" sample of just two schools, about their understandings of accountability and their views of accountability initiatives in their country and school. As was pointed out at the beginning of this Section of the report, the responses of such a small number of school practitioners clearly cannot be considered representative of school practitioners across Scotland. So this section should not be read, for example, as an evaluation of the country's evaluation policies and practices.

The purpose of this section is simply to nudge our appreciation of the meaning and consequences of accountability policies and practices in each country past the intentions captured only in official documents. It is extraordinarily rare in the history of public policy-making for everyone involved in implementing policies to hold the same view of their meaning and consequences as those who framed the set of policies to begin with.

Interviews with a total of 12 school practitioners took place in one secondary (five teachers, one school leader) and one elementary school (five teachers, one school leader).

Question 1: How do you understand the term 'accountability' in the context of your own school and classroom?

Responses to this question are summarized in relation to those people (and other entities) with whom teachers and headteachers considered themselves to have a legitimate accountability relationship.

Half of those interviewed talked about their accountability to students. All of their comments concerned student evaluation, assessment and the school's responsibility for providing a quality education. One-third of participants expressed a clear vision of the school and their duty to uphold its traditional evaluation methods and planning processes. Several teachers also mentioned their sense of responsibility to their colleagues. Participants included parents within their discussions of accountability, as well. Communication was at the forefront of their interpretation of parental accountability. For example:

"[It is our role] to maintain an open policy with parents so they are able to approach and speak to staff at any time. It is important to be accountable to parents."

Half of the interviewees outlined the government's role in establishing and evaluating accountability-driven practices. Their comments focused on the system-wide consistency of school practices and the importance of performance evaluation. A clear sense of duty was evident towards the government. Three participants mentioned that they held a sense of accountability to the community as a whole. And approximately half of the participants described their personal sense of accountability as it relates to their roles as teachers and members of the education community:

"Accountability means that I am able to justify and account for what I am teaching, why I am teaching and in some ways how I am teaching it. There are different people and groups and organizations that I am accountable to."

Question 2: Who are your clients? Who are the other stakeholders? What are some examples of their needs and wants?

In their responses to this question, interviewees identified seven different groups or other entities. All participants identified students as clients of the school and educational process. One teacher explained:

"Students want to come to a happy, threat-free school, where work attempts and efforts are valued and praised (when required) regardless of academic capability and to be taught all the basic foundations of what is required for a good start in secondary school."

Three-quarters of participants identified parents as clients or stakeholders in terms of desire for schools to meet their children's needs. Discussing school efforts to encourage parental participation in light of parental expectations, teachers stated:

"Parents are being encouraged to be more involved in their children's education; however, their expectations of what the school should do, sometimes do not sit well with the school's expectation of themselves. Most of the time parents are quite supportive."

Half of respondents felt that their colleagues were also stakeholders. Several mentioned the need for teachers to teach to the curriculum in order for their students to be prepared for the next level.

One-third of participants considered management and school level officials to be stakeholders in both the school and school system, as well:

"The management team has high standards of effectiveness about teaching and learning, record keeping, national testing results in that we get good results and that we are adding value."

Interviewees discussed a wide range of other stakeholders including local school boards, education committees, and the Education Service. About the Education Service, one teacher noted:

"The Education Service is mainly there for the benefit of clients. If it works the other way around, the system is ineffective. Also, if too much effort is required to be put into administrative work, pupils are neglected."

Future employers of current students, and the greater community were identified as stakeholders to whom accountability was due. But as several teachers pointed out, employers and schools often differ in terms of what they consider to be educational needs. One teacher explained:

"Employers have needs that are also different from what the leaders in education say that we should be giving [students]. Periodically, employers seem most interested in seeing future employees with the basics in numeracy and literacy."

Three-quarters of respondents named the government as a stakeholder in education. All of the comments about this stakeholder concerned the political nature of government interest in education. Some teachers and administrators also spoke about what they believed were discrepancies between school and government needs:

"Raising standards of achievement is certainly an important initiative; however, there is a lot of disharmony amongst teachers and the government. For example, 'Target Setting' was thrust upon us. Sometimes we would question the ways in which they are doing this. [Target Setting involves looking at socioeconomic facts and then setting targets for schools whereas perhaps they might be better set from within the school.]"

Social agencies, including social workers, doctors and therapists, were noted as stakeholders in student progress. This acknowledgment of accountability was made in light of system-wide efforts to address the needs of the whole child.

Question 3: What do you do at the present time that might be considered accountability?

In response to this question teachers and head teachers identified seven sets of practices which, from their point of view, help fulfill their accountability responsibilities. Five participants considered the performance appraisal processes in which they were involved to be an element of accountability. The majority of their comments centered around their desire to improve their teaching in the context of such appraisal. Several teachers also addressed the role that school management plays in ensuring the quality of teaching. For example:

> "Throughout the term, management will unobtrusively check that we are doing what we should be doing as in 'walking the job really,' popping into the class, speaking with the children about different topics to check up on what we are doing."

Teachers and school management associated their student evaluation practices with accountability:

> "We have a profiling system where individual pieces of work children have done with self-assessment are kept. We then compare our personal interest between teacher ideas and children ideas on areas for improvement and strength."

Half of the interviewees associated their involvement in collaborative planning activities with accountability. Although one interviewee mentioned that teachers really do not have a say in final policy or planning decisions, other teachers held a different view.

"We are developing all areas of the curriculum as part of whole-school self evaluation, where we are reviewing our practice, guidelines, policies and refining them and amending them allowing us to move along in that cyclical process. We use a development planning process."

Accountability within peer groups of teachers was mentioned several times. Teachers discussed their responsibility for ensuring that the students they pass on to their colleagues are ready to advance to the next level of their education. Nine of the interviewees included the reporting of student progress to parents as a current, accountability-driven practice. Many comments focused on creating opportunities to meet with parents to have discussions about their children's progress and their expectations. Additional forms of communication, including homework assignments that require parental assistance, were mentioned. And several teachers commented on school-based efforts to be accountable to parents for educating the whole child. For example:

"We also share things with parents as a whole school, For example, drug-awareness evening, or environmental evening, acknowledging the fact that we are responsible for the children's health in and outside of school. We are becoming more accountable for their morals, but are doing it in such a way that we share it with parents."

Question 4: What initiatives from the school-district level can you identify that seem to be aimed at increasing accountability?

Local authorities were not viewed by respondents as initiating accountability policies of their own. From the perspective of those interviewed, local authorities took up the implementation of such policies from the Scottish Office, as legally required. Three-quarters of participants associated school planning with accountability in their schools. How planning functions for purposes of accountability was explained by one interviewee this way:

"Over the last five to six years, schools have been encouraged to make plans in annual cycles to plan ahead. These plans are reviewed and are thus good examples of school-based activity reflecting accountability."

Some respondents believed however that the planning process was too driven from outside the school. In their opinion, development plans should more closely reflect staff's understandings of what the school should be attempting to do to address the needs of students.

Interviewees associated homework guidelines with accountability. As one respondent explained:

"Government and education department concern led to formulation of a homework policy, because of previous inconsistency in levels of homework. Now there are standards of what amount of homework is appropriate for different age groups."

Another initiative associated with accountability were performance indicators. One teacher described their application to increase accountability this way:

"[In this school we] just completed a baseline, broad audit of the school using performance indicators to pinpoint necessary development areas to be identified in the above development plan (all to do with accountability)."

Teachers also described, as increasing accountability, recent curriculum reviews. One teacher, for example, discussed the impact current mathematics curriculum reform was having on classroom practice:

"A number of positive results have come from this in terms of raising standards. Instead of the class teacher having students with a range of abilities in her classroom, we will group children more according to their ability. It is not streaming. It is more participative and interactive form of mathematics. It is not teacher-led and teacher-driven. It is focused on involving the children in creative math at their own level."

Several teachers identified various forms of professional development with increases in accountability. These teachers said:

> "Conferences, in-service days, discussions with colleagues do affect what you are doing in the classroom and inspire reflection which often leads to methodological changes, etc.
> In the last two weeks, the management team as a whole and teachers were at a conference looking at lifelong learning, how that could affect us in the future with secondary, primary and community education teachers sharing their skills. We also discussed increasing sharing sessions on effective teaching and being more accountable."

Teachers noted that change had recently been made in the design and wording of a new report card for parents which made it a more effective accountability tool. In addition, several teachers pointed to the link between performance appraisal and accountability in these terms:

> "Generally an audit will have been done which allows you to review and evaluate what is actually going on in the classroom, how you are carrying it out. This allows you as an individual to change your approach, content, methodology to suit the needs of individuals or the school as a whole (the audit is done in specific areas at times when it is felt appropriate).
> [The process] certainly has some influence on [classroom instruction] because if you didn't review and evaluate what you were doing and change it then you would not be meeting the needs of your clients and other relevant stakeholders. Also as an individual you need to change. You must move with the times and realize that perhaps we are more accountable now to a wider group than in the past, although probably it was always there. We were perhaps not as aware of it as we are today."

Question 5: What initiatives, from the national level can you identify that seem to be aimed at increasing accountability?

Interviewees identified national student evaluation practices as an initiative designed to increase accountability. Several teachers expressed concerns about such initiatives when excessive reliance was placed on only quantitative measures of student performance and when such measures were used for comparative purposes. One teacher suggested that the process of school planning and review was more effective in improving schools than was the comparative use of student achievement data because it produced a better understanding among staff about the goals they should be accomplishing.

Changes in methods of reporting results of student evaluations to parents also were identified as aiding accountability. One teacher explained:

"Reports have changed recently for parents. They are quite comprehensive, quite a good idea. There is also an area for the parents to get back to the teachers about anything particular they would like to address (I believe it was initiated at the local level, only for the last one to two years and will be reviewed and changed in accordance with parents feedback)."

Approximately half of the interviewees identified the five to 14 guidelines as a government accountability initiative. The school-level impact of the five to 14 initiative was commented on by several interviewees. For example, one administrator explained:

"All guidelines and policies formulated by individual schools must be aligned to these documents. Thus, we are accountable nationally across all curricular areas. This has altered some school-based activities in an improved manner e.g. continuity and progression as well as balance and structure of the curriculum have both been addressed. However, one negative outcome is that the curriculum has been narrowed in terms of depth and direct experiential learning."

Teachers also discussed the impact the five to 14 initiative has on their teaching. For example:

"On the positive side, there was a lot about the previous implementation of the curriculum that left much to be desired. For example, if a teacher was not strong in geography, students were not forced to do too much in this area if it was not a strength of theirs. However, now they are accountable and must allocate a certain percentage of time of each area of the curriculum. It is more structured."

National testing, national curriculum, target-setting, and performance indicators were other national initiatives that interviewers associated with an increase in accountability. As with most local-level accountability initiatives, these national initiatives were perceived to have both positive and negative effects.

The Netherlands

Background

The Ministry of Education, Culture and Science is responsible for elementary and secondary schools in the Netherlands. Primary education includes the years from age four through 12 with secondary education for pupils aged 12 through 18 years. Full-time compulsory education starts at age five (although most children begin at age four), and continues until the end of the year in which students reach age 16. Students are then required to attend an educational institution part-time until they are 18. The first year or two of secondary education is transitional before choosing one of four possible streams: pre-vocational, junior general secondary, senior general secondary, or pre-university. During the first three years of all secondary programs, students take 15 compulsory core curriculum courses.

The "Freedom of Education" principle (see below) is a distinguishing feature of the Netherlands approach to accountability in education. Three of the accountability initiatives described below reflect a decentralization and privatization trend, part of which is recent and part of which has evolved gradually over the past century.

Accountability policies in the Netherlands

Education Inspectorate

Although in existence for some time, in 1993 the Education Inspectorate became an autonomous organization under the Education Ministry. The Inspectorate issues a yearly "Education Report" to the Minister on the status of education in the country and this report is used by the Minister to justify his or her actions to Parliament.

Inspectors visit schools once a year, usually with prior notification. Unannounced visits are made only when serious problems are suspected (e. g., fraud or large-scale cancellation of lessons). Each year the Education Inspectorate prepares a list of priorities for each educational segment that is sent to the schools. The inspectorate has four general tasks:

- supervising compliance by schools with various statutory regulations, i.e., does the school comply with government conditions related to state funding;
- evaluating performance of schools, the quality of educational facilities, the feasibility of specific laws and regulations;
- promoting the development of the education system, particularly in the area of quality management. Among other things this entails encouraging the school to solve its own problems, to practice continuous improvement and to monitor the underlying quality of education and its organization;
- reporting to the Minister (on request or own initiative) any relevant information on the status of education.

Both schools and the inspectorate itself are accountable, given the tasks assigned to the inspectorate. Schools must provide written work plans and activity plans to the inspector: they are held accountable, at the level of justification, to parents and to the government for complying with government regulations, and for providing suitable programs and facilities. By January 1, 1999, every school must submit its School

Plan with the school's educational policy, staff policy, and internal quality assurance to the inspectorate. The inspectorate is accountable, also at the level of justification, to the government (the Minister) for development of the educational system as a whole. School evaluation reports go to schools, the Ministry, and to parliament. Reports to the Minister may result in changes to educational policy. Negative reports concerning schools can result in the loss of funds for those schools.

Choice: private schools and public finance

The "freedom of education" principle has been in the Dutch Constitution since 1848. State and private schools are funded at the same level by the government (following a 70-year public debate). All teachers have the same salary and pension rules. Public schools are run by municipal authorities and open to all children. Private schools are run by an association or foundation and can impose criteria for admission, although most pursue non-restrictive admission policies. School boards are referred to as "competent authorities." The trend is to reduce the number of state schools.

The freedom of education principle allowing school choice means that it is the responsiveness of school programs to the values, beliefs, and preferences of parents that is being accounted for. The freedom of education principle encompasses four elements:
– freedom to choose a school;
– freedom for a group to found a school, and to receive public funding for it without seeking prior government permission, providing the school enrolls a specified, minimum number of students;
– freedom to orient their school to their own religious beliefs, ideological principles or educational views (currently about 70 percent of schools are "private");
– freedom to organize the school, to choose teaching materials, and to hire staff. The Ministry does not prescribe or produce materials. But it does prescribe levels of attainment students must meet, leaving schools to decide how their students will reach those levels.
With such choice comes a greater need for public discussion of educa-

tional issues if parents are to have the information they need to make informed choices, especially if they are seeking schools for reasons other than religious beliefs.

Increased participation in decision-making

Consistent with the "freedom of education" principle, there are a large number of school boards or "competent authorities" responsible for implementing legislation/regulations and policy-making. In recent years, the trend is toward greater autonomy and decentralization. Central government powers have been increasingly confined to broad policy-making and creating the right conditions for providing "good quality education." Individual schools and local authorities have been given greater freedom in allocating resources and managing their own affairs. Secondary schools receive a block grant only, and elementary schools receive both block and targeted grants.

Although at this point municipalities have responsibilities for state schools, efforts are being made to create strongly autonomous schools able to create and implement their own policies, hire staff, acquire material, organize themselves and manage their own finances. With greater autonomy comes more responsibility to account for a greater proportion of the school's activities: no one else is responsible, at least within the framework of funding and regulations established centrally. So schools are being asked to justify what they do to parents and students more directly as parents and students participate in decisions.

Such decentralization results in loss of control by central authorities over how resources are used. Also, it requires extra effort from the inspectorate to ensure quality is maintained for all students. Theoretically at least, such decentralization should produce a school that better reflects the values, beliefs and preferences of the parents and students it serves. But as the country becomes increasingly multicultural (up to 50 percent of students in large cities are foreign-born) this policy is challenged by a need for greater integration. For central authorities, decentralization reduces the need to effectively address local issues which they are less well-positioned to understand and to address.

Participation Councils (PC)

As a further reflection of the effort to decentralize educational decision-making, the 1982 (amended 1992) Educational Participation Act requires all schools to have a Participation Council (PC). In primary schools, the PC consists of teachers, non-teaching staff, and parents (six to 18 depending on school size). In secondary schools, students also have a seat, and in upper secondary, vocational and adult education, the Council consists of staff and students only. The number of staff on the council is to equal the number of parents and/or students. Many schools also have special Parents' Councils and Student Councils to cater to the needs of specific groups. Such councils can advise the PC but have no legal powers.

PCs give parents, students and staff the right to participate in discussions and decision-making on issues relevant to the school, ranging from allocation of parent contributions to principal dismissals. Responsibility for a school's policy resides with the competent authorities, which have a duty to share their powers with the PC; together they govern the school. In addition to decisions about a wide range of school matters, the PC has a responsibility to ward off all forms of discrimination, to promote gender equity, equity for disabled persons, and an atmosphere of openness and mutual consultation in the school.

The school's Board of Governors must regularly provide the PC with updated information, meet with them at least twice yearly, and submit major decisions to the PC. The board must respond in writing within a three-month period to any proposals for the PC. The PC has advisory rights on issues such as changes in the school's religious or philosophical foundation, mergers with other schools, and holiday schedules. It has approval rights on changes in educational objectives, and the adoption of amendments to the curriculum or to the School Charter.

Every school must prepare and adopt a Participation Charter that defines the membership, organization of elections, membership duration, time within which the PC is required to produce approval or advice. Any amendments to distribution of powers are in the Charter, a copy of which is filed with the Ministry. As of August 1, 1998, a procedure for mediating disputes (the Complaints Procedure System) between the PC and school board is to be in place. Beginning January 1, 1999, schools will produce a prospectus, a School Guidebook (tool 6) to inform parents about their curriculum and the results achieved. The Central government publishes a national guide to primary education providing general information about the educational system and the rights and obligations of parents.

Attainment targets and testing

Nationally set attainment targets have been established for both primary and secondary schools. However, schools have considerable freedom to choose books and materials, and to add their own emphasis to the curriculum. For primary schools, attainment targets indicate the basic minimum that schools are required by law to teach their students in each area of the curriculum.

About 70 percent of primary schools (and increasing steadily) use a test developed by the National Institute for Educational Measurement (CITO) to assess pupils' level of attainment at the end of primary schools. Results of these or similar tests, with the head teacher's recommendation, are used to determine the appropriate type of secondary school for the pupil. For secondary schools, attainment targets describe pupil's qualities in the areas of knowledge, understanding and skills in relation to the 15 compulsory courses that comprise the secondary basic education. Secondary schools are required to ensure maximum attainment of these targets by students. At the end of basic secondary education, pupils are assessed by national (CITO) tests. Variations within the tests enable schools to respond to different learning styles and abilities, and to supplement the CITO tests with their own examinations: schools decide the test schedule. Tests do not lead to formal qualifications, but provide a basis for assessing progress toward attainment targets.

Following the period of basic education, secondary students prepare for their school-leaving examinations. The school administers internal examinations followed by exams developed and administered under central government supervision. Although currently students have a considerable choice of exam subjects, as of August 1, 1999, more stringent requirements will be in place with compulsory requirements such as a number of languages and mathematics.

Among the consequences of assessed attainment targets are revisions in national education policies, and assurance of equivalence among diplomas attained in different schools.

School prospectus

A relatively new Quality Act places the responsibility for quality achievement on the schools. One of the instruments schools will be required to use will be a prospectus. The School Plan, as this prospectus is called, is intended to inform parents about the school's educational facilities and the results that have been achieved by its students. Such plans are to help safeguard quality in the context of increasingly greater freedoms for schools in areas of policy and internal quality assurance.

The school prospectus holds the school accountable primarily to parents who are its main consumers. But plans also are submitted to the Educational Inspectorate for approval. Inspectors look at teaching methods and materials as well as how the school provides for children with special needs. School Plans are intended to increase the focus of schools on quality issues and to assist parents in the comparison of schools.

Professional standards for teachers

All teachers in the Netherlands must have at least one of three levels of teaching qualification: first-degree teachers can teach all levels of secondary education; second-degree teachers may only teach in the first three years of pre-university or senior secondary and; third-degree teachers may teach primary.

Primary teachers teach the whole curriculum, and secondary teachers a single subject. Primary degrees are earned at the Primary School Teacher College and secondary degrees at the New Teacher Training College. Both colleges offer a four-year program and university graduates have the option of attending a one-year training course to obtain the first-degree qualification.

A teacher-training process-management team currently is coordinating the reform of teacher training with an aim to developing a common curriculum for all primary teacher-training courses, a professional development plan and a regional consortia.

An October 1997 press release indicated that educational and government pressure groups had developed joint recommendations on professional standards for teachers in which they have a say in the quality-control of their profession. The release said the various educational-sectors would take on the task of forming an occupational group and developing professional standards that the group attaches to the profession and will include ethical standards and a register of teachers.

These professional standards initiatives aim to hold teacher-training institutions and the profession as a whole more accountable for ensuring that only well-qualified persons are admitted to the teaching ranks, and that experienced teachers continue to practice both ethically and effectively.

New secondary school curriculum

Beginning in the 1998–99 school year, third-year secondary students will select one of four possible educational "profiles." These alternatives include Science and Technology, Science and Health Care, Economics and Society, and Culture and Society. Within each profile, there will be a choice of three pathways – theoretical, vocational, and combined. There is also a new kind of training for direct entry to the labor market for students not capable of, or interested in, other levels. As part of this new curriculum there will be more emphasis on independent study, with the intention that in coming years schools will develop into "study houses." Within these structures students will be engaged in more independent and group work with the teacher acting in a role more like a supervisor.

School-level perspectives on accountability in the Netherlands

This section describes the results of interviews with a small number of staff members, from a "convenience" sample of just two schools, about their understandings of accountability and their views of accountability initiatives in their country and school. As was pointed out at the beginning of this Section of the report, the responses of such a small number of school practitioners clearly cannot be considered representative of school practitioners across the Netherlands. So this section should not be read, for example, as an evaluation of the country's evaluation policies and practices.

The purpose of this section is simply to nudge our appreciation of the meaning and consequences of accountability policies and practices in each country past the intentions captured only in official documents. It is extraordinarily rare in the history of public policy-making for everyone involved in implementing policies to hold the same view of their meaning and consequences as those who framed the set of policies to begin with.

Interviews with a total of 12 school practitioners took place in one secondary school (five teachers, one school leader) and one elementary school (five teachers, one school leader). In the secondary school, the headmaster and five teachers were interviewed. The headmaster, a head teacher and a teacher were interviewed in the elementary school.

Question 1: How do you understand the term accountability in the context of your own school and classrooms?

Responses to this question touched not only on the meaning of accountability as a concept, but also on what it was that respondents considered themselves accountable for. With respect to the meaning of accountability, most respondents defined it as a process of "watching over," "overseeing," "monitoring," "evaluating," "supervising" and "improving" both quality (both principals and one teacher) and efficiency (one teacher).

According to about half the respondents, this process was to be focused on the school itself, its goals, rules, and policies. For the remainder, the focus for accountability was on students, their performances, knowledge, skills, values, norms (e. g., citizenship), as well as their social and emotional development.

Only one respondent, a primary school teacher, explicitly mentioned to whom an account was owed other than education staff and students. This person spoke about the importance of informing parents about all aspects of the school's functioning.

Question 2: Who are your clients? Who are other relevant stakeholders? What are examples of their most important needs and wants?

Respondents identified as "clients," students (all respondents), parents (9), teaching colleagues (3), the school board (1), and society as a whole (1). Fourteen groups of people were identified as other "stakeholders." Six respondents again mentioned parents, while four mentioned pupils, as stakeholders. But most often identified as stakeholders (by eight respondents) were further education institutions: for interviewees in primary schools this meant secondary schools, whereas secondary school respondents included most tertiary education institutions in their responses. Others mentioned by at least several people were business and industry, neighborhoods, other schools, school boards (including the local education authority, governors and managers). Mentioned by just one respondent each were government, society as a whole, the school doctor, local police and the school advisory service.

In response to the question about the most important needs and wants of the school's clients and stakeholders, respondents noted that:
– Students want to be happy and safe at school, and receive an education adapted to their abilities.
– Parents want to see their children get a good education, make progress, and be safe and happy.
– Parents and students want students to have a good education, achieve a certificate, and develop cognitively, morally, and socially.
– Teacher training institutions want their trainees to have stimulating and productive work experiences in schools.

- Business and industry want graduates who can solve problems independently, adapt to change, and apply their skills flexibly.
- School governors want the unique features of the school to be visible to parents and the community.

Question 3: What do you do at the present time that might be considered accountability in the classroom, and with your colleagues across the school?

In response to this question, as it focused on the classroom, respondents identified three different types of actions which they associated with the meaning of accountability. One type entailed data collection from students, variously referred to as student monitoring systems, and systematic student testing programs. A second type of intervention was part of the approach taken in the school to instruction including classroom management procedures, the development of differentiated learning programs, and individualized guiding, testing, and intervention. Also part of this type of intervention were teacher-team consultations which took place concerning individual pupils, and a form of weekly planning for the work of students (diary/memo-book work) that identified their assignments for the week, among other things (most teachers in one school mentioned this).

Finally, respondents also mentioned, as a form of accountability, the assigning of homework so that parents could participate in, and monitor, the progress of their children.

With reference to school-level accountability practices, respondents identified occasions or events which reduced the autonomy of their individual decision-making, for example, classroom observation and peer assessments, team consultations, team in-service training (professionalizing the team), and collaboration among teachers within and across departments (in the secondary school).

Also associated with school-level accountability were school planning activities such as setting priorities for action for the year, development of a school prospectus, and the creation of a school work plan. Acting on the results of inspections, and consulting with school advisory services on one's work, and how to improve it, were mentioned, as well.

Teachers and principals reported accountability to be served at the school level by their school's pupil guidance system, a quality assessment process which involved regular student assessment, and a procedure in which every teacher acted as a tutor or teacher counselor.

Finally, teachers and principals in the primary school believed they were meeting expectations for accountability through advising and helping parents support their children at home.

Question 4: What initiatives from the school-district level can you identify that seem to be aimed at increasing accountability?

Respondents, whether teacher or principal, primary or secondary, were virtually unanimous in response to this question. From their perspective, the school board had virtually no influence on their work in the classroom or school.

Question 5: What initiatives from the central and local government can you identify that seem to be aimed at increasing accountability and what has been their influence on your school and classroom?

Respondents associated many more initiatives with the central government than with the local government. About half of the respondents could not identify any significant initiatives of the local government: two interviewees mentioned a compensatory education initiative, and one or two respondents each mentioned housing and accommodation, quality assurance, and road safety programs for students as local government initiatives. Among these, only quality assurance appears to qualify as an accountability initiative.

In contrast, respondents were able to identify many central government initiatives, a large proportion of them clearly counting as accountability initiatives. These included:
- a policy on school work plans,

- school inspection,
- provision of in-service training,
- efforts to improve the quality of educational leadership,
- national policy on class size reductions,
- a policy on development of the school prospectus,
- requirement for schools to have a student behavior code,
- establishment of attainment targets,
- development and implementation of large-scale innovations such as a national curriculum, study-house, learning programs, Information Communication technology,
- publication of educational documents that provide professional stimulation for educators.

Initiatives by the central government were reported to have a small number of important influences on school boards. Especially the government's large-scale innovations resulted in lump sum payments to boards to assist with implementation. This stimulated boards to engage in additional financial planning, and to take responsibility for encouraging the implementation of these large-scale innovations in schools.

Central government initiatives were associated with considerable influence at the school and classroom levels. At the school level, one outcome of such influence was described as "compliance." This meant, for example, compliance with requirements to develop a school prospectus, to have a pupil monitoring system, to create a code of student behavior, and to adopt responsibilities delegated by government to school management teams.

Government influence at the school level, however, was reported to go considerably beyond a set of perfunctory activities suggested by the term "compliance." Respondents associated the influence of the government with a number of quite positive changes in schools. For example, school prospectuses were considered by some to result in greater reflection and evaluation by staffs on their practices. As well, these prospectuses were considered by several people to provide parents with better tools for holding schools accountable. Many of the large-scale innovations introduced by government were credited with increasing the innovativeness of schools, and shaping schools' educational philosophies. The national curriculum was credited by one respondent with the retention of many students who would otherwise have dropped out of school. While many positive outcomes at the school level were associated with government initiatives, a number of teachers also pointed to considerably more work and demands on their time created by these initiatives as well as those initiatives which had an influence at the classroom level.

At the classroom level, government initiatives were also credited with significant and largely positive outcomes. In particular, the government's large-scale innovations were associated with a marked change in the forms of instruction in the classroom (strategies which promoted more active learning), additional information and examples of good classroom practice, and changes in the role of the teacher (toward facilitator and guide of the learning process). Many teachers associated government initiatives, as well, with increased in-service opportunities, more collaboration with colleagues and greater on-the-job learning. Several of the large-scale innovations directed the curriculum toward the development of skills and this created pressure for changes not only in forms of classroom instruction but approaches to student testing, as well.

Norway

Background

The documents from Norway reviewed for this study made almost no explicit reference to accountability. These documents did describe, however, initiatives related to standards and to improving performance in relation to standards.

A series of reform initiatives have been undertaken in Norway over the last few years, the most recent being the Compulsory School Reform Act introduced August 1, 1997. The purpose for this initiative was to ensure quality, coherence, and continuity of education. Elements of the reform included an increase from nine to ten years of compulsory schooling beginning at age six, and the introduction of a national curriculum for the ten compulsory years. In addition, as of 1994 all children have a right to three years of upper secondary education either in academic programs or as vocational apprenticeship training in the workplace.

Through the Ministry of Education, Research and Church Affairs, the national government determines standards and the general framework of teaching through course syllabuses and through regulating examination. The 19 counties of Norway are responsible for upper secondary education which provides the academic and vocational programs. County responsibilities include running schools, intake of students, and hiring teachers.

Municipalities are responsible for running primary and lower secondary schools, building and maintaining facilities, and hiring teachers. Preschool education is managed by a different ministry and is subject to its own set of regulations.

Accountability policies in Norway

National curricula

Reforms were introduced into the upper secondary school curriculum in 1994 and into earlier grades in 1997. The upper secondary school curriculum reforms included structural changes: reduced numbers of foundation courses; opening more places in advanced courses; content changes, with revised syllabuses for all subjects in which the specification of aims was of central importance.

The new national curriculum for grades 1 through 10 is being introduced over the three-year period beginning 1997. This curriculum consists of three parts:
- a core curriculum which is described as something to work toward and something by which progress is to measured;
- principles and guidelines for education in the compulsory school, including structure, organization and content with emphasis on communication across cultural and geographic boundaries, and gender equality;
- subject syllabuses with subject-specific aims, objectives and content.

In addition to these parts, the 1997 national curriculum is viewed as "holistic" with its four orientations. First, the curriculum is viewed as school-oriented since it lowers the school-starting age, extends compulsory education and provides a new school curriculum. Second, the curriculum is considered to be child-oriented since it makes schools responsible for providing a good developmental environment, and a wealth of opportunities for learning and play in various activities with adults in different roles. The curriculum is viewed, third, as family-oriented also since it encourages collaboration with home, school, local community, and expansion of after-school activities for child safety while parents work. Finally, the curriculum is oriented toward cultural reform with its emphasis on the aesthetic dimension and the need to learn about different cultures.

The 1997 national curriculum is said to reflect the "one school for all" principle, and balances considerations for the community and adapted education for the individual. The new curriculum places greater emphasis on common subject matter while giving room for local and individual adjustment. A Saami curriculum (the heritage of a minority originally living in the north) is coordinated with, and considered equal to, the national curriculum.

These new curricula are holding schools and individual teachers more accountable, at the level of justification, for a wider range of outcomes than was the case previously. This account is owed to students, parents and the local community. One consequence of providing this account is more transparency with respect to the school's responsibilities. It is not clear what the additional understanding on the part of students, parents and the local community potentially resulting from such transparency might lead to, however. The national curriculum also may produce some tension between national and local needs.

Student assessment in primary and lower secondary education (gr. 1–10)

New regulations related to assessment were introduced in the Compulsory School Reform Act in October 1997. Previous practices were strengthened with clearer guidelines for planning and implementation. Assessment is intended to reflect the aims and objectives of the national core curriculum and subject syllabuses. Its purpose is to judge whether or not progress has been made in relation to these objectives, and to decide how to achieve better results.

The most important purpose for assessment is to promote pupils' learning and development. It should do this by encouraging pupils to use their abilities and aptitudes. It should do this, as well, by providing information about what the pupil has learned, and by contributing to communication and cooperation between schools and pupils' homes. Further, as Norwegian policy-makers envision assessment, it should help teachers and schools to improve the quality of their teaching and adapt it to the needs of individual pupils.

Assessment is to be carried out with and without grades. Assessment without grades provides guidance for the student while conveying what the pupil has been taught, taking into account individual differences and contributing to motivation and comprehension. In addition to assessments made in daily teaching, the teacher is required to meet with parents/guardians at least twice a year for planned and structured talks that conclude with agreement on areas for concentration. Teachers are advised to include students in this conversation. The talks will inform pupils and parents about the pupil's learning and development, give guidance for future work, and provide the teacher with a better basis to adapt the teaching to the needs of the individual student. The Ministry, through Reform 97, aims to systematize this assessment by developing diagnostic tests with guidelines and handbooks showing teachers how to evaluate the results to improve conditions uncovered.

Assessment with grades will be conducted in the lower secondary grades using a 1–6 scale (same as used for upper secondary students). End-of-term grades are to be accompanied by teachers' comments and guidance, oral in some cases and written in others.

Primary and intermediate students will be assessed only without grades and lower secondary will be assessed both with and without grades using the two forms to supplement each other. During the ten compulsory years of schooling, students are to move automatically to the next grade. In the last term of the tenth year, students will complete a major project for which a teacher's comment will appear on the pupil's Leaving Certificate.

At the end of grade 10 there is a final written examination. Each student takes at least one exam. The teachers in the school prepare the exam, but selection of a sample of students to do a particular exam and marking are done externally.

This assessment system appears to be designed largely to hold students accountable, at the level of justification, to teachers and parents. Such a system has the potential to guide teachers' instruction and students' curricular choices (e. g., selecting area of study and admission in school of choice for upper secondary school). It should keep parents reasonably well-informed of their child's progress, as well.

Student assessment in upper secondary education
(non-compulsory three to four years past grade 10)

At this level pupil evaluation is intended to inform pupils, parents, teachers and the school as a whole about the pupil's progress in relation to the course objectives. Such evaluation also is intended to serve as a tool for the guidance, motivation and development of the pupil, and to offer teachers an opportunity to continuously evaluate their teaching procedures. Providing information to the larger society, employers, and higher education about the competence of the pupil is also a purpose for such evaluation.

Both continuous and final evaluation are used with two types of marks recorded on student certificates: overall achievement on various types of work through the year, and end-of-year examinations in written subjects that are organized by public examination bodies and evaluated centrally by groups of experienced teachers.

Pupils are being held accountable, at the level of justification, for their achievement. They are accounting to themselves, their parents, future employers and institutions of higher education, with bearing on employment and higher education opportunities. As well, teachers are being held accountable for the quality of their instruction, specifically its contribution to their students' achievement. Such accountability, however, appears to be voluntary with no explicit consequences.

Decentralization of decision-making

In Norway, decentralization means giving the local education authorities more discretion. The national government, for example, now gives counties block grants rather than funding all education directly. Decentralization, in this context, does not mean devolution of control to the school, although gradual increases in the professional autonomy of individual schools is claimed. Counties, municipalities, and schools are encouraged to develop some aspects of the school curriculum to reflect a local focus.

There is a nine-member National Parents' Committee for Primary and Lower Secondary Education whose responsibilities are not defined. Some municipalities have a Municipal Parents' Council as a coordinating body for all schools in the municipality.

Each school has a Parents' Council of which all parents are members. This council meets at least twice each year to elect representatives, to assume some responsibility for planning class leisure activities, and to serve as the primary contact between teachers and parents. Such meetings also are an opportunity to discuss issues of concern and to hear about school programs and activities. Each parent council elects a Working Committee, and two council members represent the parents on the School Board which is advisory to school leaders.

Pupils have their own Pupils' Council with the same level of representation on internal committees and the School Board as their parents. National goals stress the importance of this participation in the development of democratic citizens and for providing a forum for student views. Students are also expected to participate in Class Councils to learn how to be active in their communities as part of the Reform 97 curriculum. The work of Pupil and Class Councils is mostly linked to the general running of the school.

The multiple facets of decentralization and decision participation in Norway create a complex set of accountability relationships (at the level of justification) rather than a "clear line" of accountability. Such complexity, however, mirrors reasonably well the actual network of influences on the success of students at school. Parents, students, teachers and governing bodies all make well-known and significant contributions to such success. The consequences of this approach to accountability help to ensure that students and parents have the opportunity to be well-informed of school programs, and in a modest way to directly influence their design.

Open school boundaries

Primary, intermediate, and lower secondary students in Norway generally attend the public school in that part of the municipality closest to their home (the private school-sector is very small). Emphasis is given to the principle of an "all-inclusive school," one in which all pupils receive an equitable education based on a common curriculum with suitable local adaptations. Schools are expected to make use of resources in the local community and to be a center for local activities.

At the upper secondary level, pupils have the right to apply for courses at any school in their own or a neighboring municipality. The tradition of ensuring that pupils in all parts of the country have access to the same opportunities, with similar standards for all schools, results in the choice of school largely being dictated by the pupil's course of study priorities. Authorities are obliged by law to fulfill one of the student's three choices and over 90 percent of students are claimed to get their first choice.

Upper secondary schools are accountable to parents and students for providing a description of their programs so that suitable choices can be made by students. These upper secondary schools need to be very clear about their programs to avoid attracting students with false expectations about their courses.

Primary, intermediate, and lower secondary schools are accountable, at the level of justification, to the government, as well as to students and parents, for being inclusive. There does not seem to be an explicit mechanism for demonstrating such inclusiveness. Presumably, however, widespread dissatisfaction with a school could lead to reduced enrollment, academically weaker students, or an increase in the private alternatives within a municipality.

National evaluation system

An initiative to develop a national evaluation system is underway in response to a perceived need to have more information at the national level about numbers of pupils, competence of teachers, student achievement, and how the different parts of the system are functioning. The main elements of this future national system of evaluation are:
- School-based evaluation: Although local school development programs are a requirement of local curriculum planning and strategic institutional planning, the National Ministry has developed a handbook to assist teachers and school administrators in school-based evaluation. Through the county National Education Offices, the Ministry intends to provide funds to raise competence in the conduct of such evaluation. Municipalities are responsible for ensuring that such evaluations are carried out. As of Reform 97, primary, intermediate and lower secondary schools are required by law on a regular basis to assess the extent to which organization and implementation of educational activities are aligned with curriculum objectives.
- Educational statistics: National Education Offices are expected to collect data in their regions for the Ministry and distribute results. Current statistics on time spent in different activities, number of student, schools, personnel, and examination results/marks will be supplemented with teacher qualifications and economic conditions. A National report is planned.
- Examinations: A National Examination Board will work to improve the exams. Information on student performance will be used for selecting areas for diagnostic testing or other surveys and evaluations.
- Assessments of pupils' learning: As noted above, the informal evaluation will be emphasized and systematized. Diagnostic tests along with guidelines and handbooks developed by the Ministry and edu-

cational experts will help teachers evaluate their test results and better use them in local development work.

– Information on contexts for learning and area evaluations: National objectives have been designed to improve "contexts" beginning with educational leadership, home-school relationship, and the organization of educational activities. Evaluations in specific areas is expected to help inform policy-making.

Once fully developed, the national evaluation system will provide the means for holding schools and municipalities more precisely accountable to parents, students, and the national government for student outcomes and for creating the educational conditions that help students accomplish such outcomes.

Professional standards for teachers

Teachers may become qualified in several different ways in Norway. After several years of consultation and planning, teacher education reform is being implemented in the fall of 1998 and a new model of vocational training will be introduced gradually between 2000 and 2006. Teachers of general or academic studies normally are qualified to teach in two or three different subjects and teachers of vocational subjects must have full trade qualifications and teach the subjects of their trade. The changes will require:

– three years consecutive study for preschool teachers,
– four years consecutive study of general subjects for class teachers at primary and lower secondary levels (general teachers education),
– four years consecutive study (starting 1999) for specialized subject teachers in subjects like arts and crafts, drama, music, and nutrition/home economics (nutrition, health, and environmental subjects),
– decentralized study programs (all main types of teacher education except specialist subject teacher education),
– professional competence as an artist with one additional year of education theory and practice,
– lower or higher university or college degree, and one year of educational theory and practice.

Certification of teachers is on the basis of an officially recognized exam in an authorized institution. There is no mandatory, organized, supervision of teachers after completion of teacher education, and there is no period of probation for teachers. Dismissal of teachers is rare.

Practicing teachers are expected to take in-service training but opportunities to do so appear to vary with the availability of resources within the local authority. However, there are expected to be more efforts to provide in-service in the current context of new initiatives.

School-level perspectives on accountability in Norway

This section describes the results of interviews with a small number of staff members, from a "convenience" sample of just two schools, about the their understandings of accountability and their views of accountability initiatives in their country and school.

A total of 12 teachers and principals participated in the interviews. At the elementary school, the principal and six teachers shared their thoughts on accountability in schools. The secondary school principal and four secondary teachers also participated.

Question 1: How do you understand the term accountability in the context of your own school and classrooms?

Interviewees described accountability in terms of the individuals and groups towards whom their felt a sense of responsibility. All but one of the participants mentioned students when addressing their perception of the term "accountability." Teachers and administrators also expressed their sense of duty towards the reporting of student progress, attendance and achievement. Within their discussions of accountability, 20 percent of participants mentioned their colleagues. 60 percent of participants remarked on their sense of duty towards their principals or school level administrators. Their comments were focused on their need to report on their professional development, as well as that of their students.

106

While parents were mentioned by half of the interview participants, teachers and administrators restricted their comments to the importance of teacher-parent relationships. Several teachers also addressed every educator's responsibility and obligation to the parents of students that had not yet attained the age of majority.

Teachers and administrators remarked on their responsibility to adhere to curriculum and student-based legislation enacted by the government. As well, 40 percent of participants highlighted the role of the educational funding bodies in ensuring accountability is achieved. As one teacher said:

> "We have to report to the authorities that are providing money. We received lump sums and we are accountable for how the moneys are used within the frames decided by the authorities. Budgetary details are reported to the district and the buffer numbers are reported to the central authorities."

One teacher also addressed the changing perception and acceptance of systematic accountability initiatives:

> "There is more openness about these issues now than before. This is a positive development."

Question 2: Who are your clients? Who are other relevant stakeholders? What are examples of their most important needs and wants?

The most frequently mentioned school-level client and stakeholder groups were students and parents. They were highlighted by 90 and 70 percent of participants, respectively. While half of the interview participants included local politicians, 40 percent mentioned school leaders in their discussions of stakeholders in the educational system.

There was a clear distinction between how participants' interpreted educational clients and stakeholders. While client groups were listed as students, parents, society, principals, teacher colleagues and school authorities, participants had a different interpretation of stakeholder groups. The stakeholder groups included local politicians, school leaders, the Ministry, and society. Parents, higher education institutions and future employers were also included as interested parties in the educational process.

With respect to student needs and wants, over half of the participants highlighted the importance of students being "comfortable" at school and "having a good time." As student support and evaluator, one teacher added:

> "My job is to give the best education possible to as many students as possible, but also to evaluate and rank the pupils to meet the needs of higher education and society."

When addressing the needs and wants of parents, 30 percent of teachers commented on parents' desires to receive information about the school, their children and their classroom activities. Two secondary teachers highlighted grades and student ranking as something of great interest to parents, as well.

90 percent of participants elaborated on the needs and wants of school level authorities. Participants remarked on the need for the national and local educational authorities to be informed about school activities and achievement. Several participants also commented on the discrepancies between the interests of the politicians and the reality in the schools. The most commonly associated need was described by one teacher as follows:

> "The educational authority wants to know to which degree goals are achieved in accordance with political and educational decisions in both the legal acts and the national curriculum."

Several teachers also highlighted the national and local authority's expectations for teachers to "do their best in accordance with the National Curriculum."

Question 3: What do you do at the present time that might be considered accountability according to this definition?

Participants identified three of their current practices as accountability driven. Subject matter plans and work plans were highlighted as two means to improve teaching. Two secondary teachers also identified student feedback about one's teaching as a form of accountability. One elementary teacher commented:

> "[My teaching efforts] get reported to the principal through teacher appraisals and class visits made by the principal and assistant principal."

80 percent of participants mentioned current student evaluation and reporting practices as current accountability-driven initiative. Teachers frequently mentioned their role in allocating marks for student work and achievement. Similarly, several teachers commented on their efforts to work together to improve their reporting efforts, the fairness of their judgements, in particular. Other teachers commented on their responsibility to report on "students with special needs" and to "report on student achievement to parents."

Half of the interviewees associated accountability with such school level initiatives as school development planning, curriculum planning (reported to the local authorities), evaluation questionnaires administered to all first-year students about curriculum and its implementation, and annual school reports highlighting issues selected by the regional board.

Question 4: What initiatives from the school-district level can you identify that seem to be aimed at increasing accountability?

About the role of regional authorities in accountability, participants discussed the nature of the hierarchical flow of demands for greater accountability and identified four distinct accountability-based initiatives. One of these was teacher evaluation. While 95 percent of participants commented on regional accountability initiatives aimed at influencing teacher performance, their comments addressed a variety of issues. And teachers were divided on the success of current initiatives. About a third of the interviewees considered reporting measures to be time-consuming. This erodes time available for teaching and preparation for teaching without improving that teaching.

> "But several teachers were more optimistic about the effects of such initiatives as the work documents plans which, they believed, increased one's reflection on one's teaching and other activities in the school. Several teachers also noted the positive student-related impact on students of teacher accountability initiatives by, for example increasing the contact between pupils and teachers."

The administrative requirements of these accountability initiatives, however, were considered by 40 percent of interviewees to be excessively time-consuming.

A second set of accountability initiatives associated with regional authorities by over half of the elementary teachers were standardized testing and the new national curriculum. Reaction to these changes appeared to be neutral among most participants, although one teacher complained about not enough information resulting from these efforts to be of much help in improving classroom practice.

School level documentation and comparison was a third set of regional accountability initiatives identified by about a quarter of respondents. School development plans, annual reports and student questionnaires were mentioned.

Finally, one administrator noted that there is a "public revision of economic matters done at least every second year."

Question 5: What initiatives from the government level can you identify that seem to be aimed at increasing accountability?

Participants discussed the implications of four different nationally controlled accountability initiatives. Teacher reporting was the first of these. 90 percent of participants highlighted the impact of increasing demands for documentation on all aspects of teacher work. For example:

"The amount of reflection upon our own teaching has considerably increased as a result of the changes.
There is a strongly felt demand on documentation and focus on what and how evaluations and reports are supposed to be done. Many teachers are now working very conscientiously and are reporting with caution."

School-level reporting required by the government was characterized by 40 percent of teachers and administrators in a manner illustrated by these remarks:

"There is an influence on the daily life in the school at various levels. There are piles of forms to be completed. They come from the top of the hierarchy and flow down through the system.
Sometimes I feel that they ask for reports just as an exercise in filling in forms."

Pupil boards were another accountability initiative of the government identified by respondents. An administrator at the secondary school had the following comments on the pupils board:

"It is very positive and is trying to motivate the pupils to participate in all sorts of evaluation but I am sorry to say that there are pupils that do not understand that this is for their own good.
It is an important pedagogical challenge to educate for democratic and human rights. The pupils need to be trained in these matters."

There was much discussion, among those interviewed, about the legal aspects of national accountability initiatives. Several teachers mentioned the increased role the national level is playing in decision-making and guiding the curriculum. Several teachers explained:

"The provision of the act says that all schools are obliged to continuously evaluate their activities and report accordingly.

The assessment law and the curriculum are decided by the politicians at the national level and we all have to obey.

The teachers mandate is based on the laws and curriculum decided by our national assembly."

Canada (Province of Ontario)

Background

The provinces and territories of Canada are assigned responsibility for elementary and secondary education in the Canadian constitution. In theory, educational policy and practice in these different Canadian jurisdictions could be radically different. In practice, this is rarely the case in any area of educational policy and practice, including those concerned with accountability. So, while it is a sample of Ontario accountability policies and practices described in this section of the paper, most of what appears here can be found in other parts of Canada in some closely approximate form.

Indeed, the response to calls for greater accountability in education were resisted longer in Ontario than in most other provinces and territories.

But resistance has been replaced with enthusiasm in the past three years, and the current high priority given to accountability is best exemplified by the recent appearance of a new agency, the Education Quality and Accountability Office (EQAO). Established in February 1995, EQAO is an "arms length" government agency reporting directly to the Minister of Education and Training with a mandate to:

- develop tests, and manage their administration in cooperation with school boards;
- evaluate the results and report them to the public;
- make recommendations to the government to improve the quality of education;

- manage Ontario's participation in international testing;
- conduct research on best classroom practices;
- collect quantitative and qualitative data to evaluate the effectiveness of the educational system;
- report publicly each year on testing results and related system evaluation.

Accountability policies in Canada (Ontario)

Student testing

The most prominent EQAO accountability strategies and tools depend on student testing. A second, less prominent tool (one not yet implemented) is the development of an indicators system. EQAO has introduced province-wide student testing into Ontario at both elementary and secondary school levels. While common in many other Canadian provinces and other countries, such testing had not been part of Ontario practice, with the exception of grade 13 exit exams discontinued some 15 years ago.

In the spring of 1997, an annual, performance-based test of all grade 3 (130000) students in the province was initiated in the areas of reading, writing and mathematics. In this first year, testing occurred over ten days within the context of a variety of teacher-supervised classroom activities. This time allocation was reduced by half during the second year of administration.

The tests generally are administered during the spring term and marked over the summer when the data are compiled and analyzed. In the fall of each year, individual reports are sent home to parents and the EQAO releases a provincial report along with recommendations for improvement. Schools and school boards release their reports and are expected to begin working on action plans for improvement.

A sample of the province's grade 6 students were tested in mathematics in 1995 and 1997 and will be tested in reading and writing in 1999, and in mathematics in 2001. A sample of grade 9 students was tested in mathematics in 1998 and will be tested in a yet to be determined subject in 2000. Every grade 10 student in the province will be given a literacy test, but the details on scheduling have yet to be developed.

On all of these tests the students' work is graded according to 4 levels of performance, based on provincial standards and curriculum, with levels 2 to 3 being the expected range for most students.

Like its counterparts in other provinces and countries, no attempt yet has been made by EQAO to adjust test scores to account for differences in socio-economic conditions, family education cultures, and other factors known to explain substantial amounts of the variation in student achievement.

With full public disclosure of student test results aggregated to the school and district-level, student testing in Ontario is "high stakes" for schools, with accounts largely intended for parents and the public at large. The media regularly report these results with comparisons across districts, and within districts across schools. Districts and schools are left with the task of explaining and justifying their results.

Because many large urban and suburban districts in Ontario have open boundary policies, one potential consequence of this high stakes testing is loss or gain in individual school enrollment. Certainly, the publicity surrounding the reporting of test results ensures that these results capture the attention of teachers and school administrators. But there is very little systematic knowledge (but considerable speculation) about what is the impact of that attention. Those advocating such testing programs typically assume that they will produce increased efforts by teachers and administrators to improve their school's effectiveness as defined by official curriculum policy.

Educational Indicators Program

Another responsibility of the EQAO has been to develop a comprehensive Education Quality Indicators Program (EQUIP) that will produce profiles of schools, boards and the province, and include information that will complement and support interpretation of assessment data. When implemented, the EQUIP will

- provide a comprehensive and readily-understood picture of Ontario education,
- ensure student achievement is reported in the proper context,
- establish a sound basis for program improvement efforts.

Following a consultation period with opportunity for input from parents, teachers, students, administrators and officials, and the public, a list of indicators will be selected and a "pilot test" of the indicator program conducted in September of 1998.

Standardized report card

New, standard, elementary and secondary province-wide report cards were introduced by the Ministry August 27, 1997. The elementary school report card, to be issued three times per year, was phased in over the 1997–98 school year in 30 percent of schools. It is to be implemented in all schools in the 1998–99 school year. A new standard secondary school report card will be introduced starting in grade 9, in September 1999.

Both new report cards are aligned with the new provincial curricula (described below). Students in grades 1 to 6 receive letter grades while grades 7 and 8 students receive percentages as well as grade averages. The letters and percentages are expected to reflect student performance in relation to specific levels of achievement used in Ministry curriculum. Teachers are expected to understand and apply these levels as they assess student achievement throughout the year.

The report card holds students accountable to their parents by describing their progress in relation to curriculum-prescribed standards. To the extent that the report card leads to interaction among teachers, students, and parents, the report card becomes a vehicle for explaining the curriculum, and justifying the student's progress. The card is intended to provide parents with clear, concise information about their child's progress throughout the school year. In this way, the Ministry expects that parents will be better informed about how their children are doing and in a better position to become full partners in their children's education.

Student-targeted provincial funding formula

In March of 1998, the government announced a new student-targeted approach to funding intended to increased the accountability of school boards. These measures are described by the provincial government as matching the accountability emphasis created by EQAO's student testing initiatives. The government has targeted how the money is to be spent, with some flexibility allowed for local priorities.

The Ministry will develop a Standard School Board Financial Report Card that school boards will be required to use to report their financial performance and that of individual schools. The report will show clearly what a board's estimated budget was and how much was actually spent outside the classroom. A summary will be issued of what each school board has spent to inform parents and taxpayers of their spending decisions.

School districts are being asked to explain their spending priorities and patterns to the government, parents, and other taxpayers. It is not yet clear what would be the consequences for a school district of not conforming to government-prescribed funding patterns and priorities. The Ministry expects "parent and taxpayer satisfaction will improve in comparison with prior-year experience."

New elementary school curriculum

A new curriculum was introduced for elementary schools in 1997. This curriculum was intended to be the centerpiece of the province's education reform which is designed to improve student achievement and increase accountability to parents in the education system. The grade 1 to 8 curriculum was described as "rigorous and challenging," spelling out exactly what children should learn in each and every grade. Children are expected to read, write and spell at an earlier age and have sharper problem-solving skills, according to the new curriculum.

Math and language curricula were introduced in the fall of 1997, with the remaining curricula to be introduced in 1998.

Secondary school reform

A significant number of changes are being introduced into Ontario secondary schools at the present time and while their purposes are many and varied, most aim to increase the accountability of secondary schools, one way or another. Central among these changes are new, rigorous, curricula. These curricula are intended to embody high graduation standards for all students; provide clear course requirements for students planning to go to university, college or workplace; introduce clearer means of reporting to parents; to expand co-op education and work experience programs; and to improve guidance and career counseling policies and programs. These curricula place greater emphasis on math, science and language throughout the secondary program. Students will also be required to pass a grade 10 literacy test before graduation. Curriculum documents for the new four-year secondary program are to be released for use in September 1999.

Other components of the secondary reform program (in addition to the literacy test) announced in January 1997 are:
- reintroduction of streaming for the four high school years (in response to requests from parents and teachers);
- more compulsory courses based on representations from parents, teachers, students and business;
- 40 hours of community involvement;
- establishment of a Provincial Partnership Council of representatives from government, education, business and the voluntary sector. Members are appointed by the Minister to help expand co-op education, work experience, school-to-work and community involvement programs and increase private-sector participation in them;
- a teacher-advisor system for students in grades 7 to 11 to monitor a student's progress and by a key school contact for parents;
- a prior learning assessment process that allows a student to receive a credit without taking a course if they can demonstrate mastery of high provincial standards.

The College of Teachers (COT) was established in July 1996 to regulate and govern the teaching profession. It also claims to have elevated teaching to a self-regulating profession, functioning as a professional college with authority to license, govern and regulate the practice of teaching. The COT assumes responsibility for developing standards of teaching practice, regulating on-going teacher certification and professional development, and accrediting teacher education programs.

The motivation for establishing COT was to make the teaching profession more accountable to the public by having members of the public on the Council and all committees of the College, as well as having all meetings open to everyone. Public accountability is seen to be the key to teacher discipline and, therefore, to remove the appearance of a conflict of interest. Responsibility for teacher discipline was transferred from the province's teachers' federations to the college.

With regard to standards of practice the COT:

— sets standards to define what teachers should know and be able to do at each stage of their career;
— sets standards for graduation from accredited pre-service and in-service teacher education programs;
— monitors teacher education programs to ensure compliance with the standards;
— develops a process to improve preparation and support for associate teachers working with beginning teachers.

COT is expected to play a major role in developing a provincial framework for professional learning, with the objective of helping teachers obtain the training they need to support them in their jobs, and to implement new government policies and programs. The College has the authority to regulate teaching qualifications, set membership criteria, enroll members and create a provincial register of teachers. It is responsible, as well, for investigating complaints involving members, conducting hearings into allegations of professional misconduct, and taking appropriate disciplinary action.

In 1987, the provincial government established the Education Improvement Commission. The purpose of the Commission is to oversee the amalgamation and development of new (larger) district school boards, to clarify the role of school board trustees, and strengthen the involvement of parents and their communities in their schools. The first two tasks have been completed with the reduction in the number of school boards in Ontario by about a half, and the Commission's support of a strong, continuing role for elected trustees and school boards.

The provincial guidelines for school council operations are set out in a policy memorandum issued in 1996. In 1997, the Minister indicated the government wished to establish a strong role for school councils. They would continue to provide advice on how to deliver the best education for students, but under the restructured system with larger boards, they would have a stronger advisory role in areas of program offerings, discipline, and reporting on academic progress. The Commission is currently consulting with the public and conducting research on the future role of school councils, the results of which will be reported by the end of 1998. In the meantime, 1996 guidelines remain in place.

School-level perspectives on accountability in Canada (Ontario)

This section describes the results of interviews with a small number of staff members, from a "convenience" sample of just two schools, about their understandings of accountability and their views of accountability initiatives in their country and school. As was pointed out at the beginning of this Section of the report, the responses of such a small number of school practitioners clearly cannot be considered representative of school practitioners across Ontario. So this section should not be read, for example, as an evaluation of the country's evaluation policies and practices.

The purpose of this section is simply to nudge our appreciation of the meaning and consequences of accountability policies and practices in each country past the intentions captured only in official documents.

Interviews were conducted with a total of 12 people at one elementary (K-5) and one middle (grade 6–8) school. Five teachers and the principal from each school participated in the interviews.

Question 1: How do you understand the term accountability in the context of your own school and classroom?

Teachers and administrators described their thoughts on accountability in terms of both individual and group participants in the education system.

Discussing their thoughts on educational accountability, all those interviewed noted their sense of responsibility towards their students. Promoting student success and maintaining accurate records were highlighted as important accountability practices. Several teachers mentioned their commitment to ensuring that all students' needs are met.

Interviewees noted the importance of meeting provincial and board level expectations, and implementing new programs. One teacher also mentioned his/her sense of accountability towards the curriculum. Both teachers and administrators mentioned parents in their discussions of accountability. Advocating for students, providing the best possible learning experiences, and maintaining open lines of communication were highlighted as important elements of accountability to parents.

And as one teacher said, "We are accountable to ourselves. We have chosen to do this job and we want to be good at it."

Question 2: Who are your clients and other relevant stakeholders? What are their needs and wants?

Participants unanimously agreed that students were their most important clients. There was a slight division between the elementary and secondary participants in terms of their perception of student needs. While all participants felt that student success was important, elementary participants focused their comments on each student's need to feel secure and gain self-esteem, as well. But one teacher described how current provincial changes are influencing his/her perceptions of accountability to students:

"In the past, I would have said that my accountability was student driven. Now this year, it is top down. Instead of being accountable to student needs I am accountable to the Ministry directives. I am accountable to report how students measure up against those standards."

While all elementary participants felt that parents were clients, as well, only half of the secondary participants echoed this view. Secondary participants were more likely to identify with parents as stakeholders. It was clear that interviewees sensed parental need for open communication with teachers and the school. Elementary participants also discussed the need for parents to have opportunities to participate in school activities and receive substantiated information about their child's progress.

The school and school colleagues were mentioned as significant stakeholders in the educational process along with community groups and society as a whole. Increases in community participation and communication within the schools were seen as positive steps towards greater accountability.

One teacher added:

"There are long-term implications for the community. We are raising tomorrow's future. We need to give students what they need."

Interviewees emphasized the importance of the links between social service agencies and schools. Both administrators highlighted the importance of school accountability towards these groups.

Question 3: What do you do at the present time that might be considered accountability according to this definition?

When asked to identify their current accountability-based practices, participants discussed five different initiatives. The first of these was evaluation. Respondents often explained how traditional teacher and student evaluation practices were accountability driven. Along these lines, most participants outlined their practice of recording student progress and achievement. Teachers also referred to the current provincial curricular changes and their influence on student evaluation. Some teachers felt that the newest version of the curricular evaluation expectations were more clearly stated. The provincial standardized testing practices were also highlighted.

Interviewees spoke, secondly, of their sense of responsibility towards improving student achievement. Participants championed their responsibility for creating safe learning environments and addressing individual student needs. In relation to curriculum, several teachers claimed that their teaching had become more directly influenced by the provincial curriculum than had been the case in the past.

One school administrator explained that, "My role is to maintain the good climate but to work at greater academic accountability and improve the achievement."

Third, although collaboration with colleagues was not mentioned by any of the elementary participants, all secondary participants described the impact and importance of their collaborative efforts. For example:

"I am constantly sharing with other teachers and getting feedback on my teaching.
I get together with colleagues to look at current curriculum demands and how to best present them. We also look at curriculum units for the month.
I teach workshops for other teachers on new curriculum and accountability."

Communication with parents was identified as a fourth accountability-oriented practice by interviewees. Report cards were highlighted as

122

important tools for sharing information with parents. Although secondary teachers mentioned the importance of communicating with parents, elementary teachers focused on the methods they use to promote parental involvement. For example:

"We write a weekly book [of student activities] that goes home to parents each week. Parents, in turn, have to sign the book and comment."

A sixth accountability-related practice identified by respondents was school planning. The importance of school and personal goals was frequently mentioned. Most people mentioned the influence of the professional development components of their school plans. Teachers also talked about the importance of school goals and plans reflecting the school district goals and plans.

Question 4: What initiatives from the school district-level can you identify that seem to be aimed at increasing accountability?

Participants identified two board level initiatives that were designed to improve teacher and school-level accountability. The first of these was curriculum. Respondents discussed how the district creates opportunities for teachers to participate in decision-making around curriculum and other important issues. Many teachers also mentioned the role the district plays in providing resource documents and support for teachers. One teacher commented:

"Teachers are kept very well-informed and on top of things. Teachers are asked about and plan board approaches to dealing with educational change and curriculum issues."

Half of interviewees associated the district's professional development activities with accountability. Specifically mentioned were professional development initiatives related to special education, the new provincial report card, and train-the-trainer approaches by the district for providing in-service in schools on other matters. Several teachers also commented on the degree of autonomy schools have to create their own professional development activities.

Question 5: What initiatives from the government can you identify that seem to be aimed at increasing accountability?

Participants described five different provincially-based accountability initiatives. One of these was student reporting. Although many participants acknowledged the new provincial report card as an accountability tool, it met with mixed reviews. Several teachers commented on the positive changes brought about by the new report card. For example:

"I strongly support the report card and the new curriculum. It makes us all more accountable.
It is a good improvement over the old report card and it is meeting with positive response.
It provides better information for parents."

Other participants shared their skepticism about the report cards:

"The new report card does not really change accountability because we have always had to support our assessment of students with data. Now we have different categories to partition them into.
The card has four levels of achievement. It's hard to evaluate kids and put them into the different categories."

Teachers also expressed their feelings about the lack of preparation and support, from the Ministry, to assist them with their transition to the new, computerized, report card.

The establishment of the College of Teachers was seen as a provincial accountability initiative by many respondents, who also noted that current accountability initiatives occasionally make teachers more aware of provincial standards and expectations.

All elementary teachers discussed the government's (EQAO's) grade 3 testing program. They disagreed on the impact of this program, however. Those supporting such testing said, for example:

"There has been a positive effect on teachers. And there has been a positive effect on student outcomes.
With the new evaluation system, everyone [teachers, parents and students] is more aware of what is needed to succeed."

But some respondents worried about the dangers of standardized testing and its potential impact on their students and school:

"There will be potentially negative impacts on the schools that have needy children because their scores will be lower.
Some educators see value in the testing because parents can compare their kids. But, it will end up destroying their children's self-esteem.
This approach will widen the socioeconomic differences even more. There is also less time for activities ... getting away from the fun things.
Teachers are often teaching to the test."

Participants also expressed their feelings about current funding practices that have included cuts to education funding. The elementary level interviewees expressed concerns for their students and their school's programs. Some interviewees also noted the impact funding cuts are having on professional development and school programming. One administrator explained:

"Teachers are feeling that there is less support because consultants and workshops have been cut. Our school's major concerns are with staffing and resources because our school is so high in special education and English as a second language. We know cuts are coming in those areas. We are worried about how to provide the best support."

While several participants commented on the impact school councils had on their schools, their comments were limited to the increased communication between parents and the school.

New Zealand

Background

In 1989 the New Zealand government's *Tomorrow's School* policy introduced a major restructuring of the school system that focused on governance in the form of school-based management. The 1989 act covered all schools, both state and independent (private). Current reforms are more about setting standards for students, teachers and principals. In addition to accountability tools currently in place, there are several consultations underway related to potential new policies.

Schooling is compulsory for all children from their sixth to their 16th birthday, although most start school on their fifth birthday. Compulsory education is divided into primary, intermediate or middle, and secondary schooling. Primary schools are for children in Year 0 (age five) to Year 6. Students in their 7th and 8th Year may be either in a separate intermediate school or part of a primary, secondary, or composite/area school. Secondary schools are for students from Year 9 to Year 13.

Recently there has been a growth in programs for the Maori students with growing numbers enrolled in bilingual and Maori language immersion classes within mainstream schools. As well, New Zealand has a significant and growing Pacific Island population whose students have lower levels of achievement than other students. As a result, a formal education plan is being developed to improve education for island students.

126

Accountability policies in New Zealand

School-based management

Prior to October 1, 1989 administration of New Zealand schools was under the control of the Department of Education and education boards in a structure described as "complex and centralized." With the introduction of the Tomorrow's School policy, schools were given the responsibility for their own management, in partnership with the community, through a board of trustees which includes elected parent and community volunteers, the principal, and a staff representative. Secondary school boards also have a student representative. Independent schools are controlled by committees, trustee boards, and management boards on behalf of the owners.

School boards establish a charter which sets out the aims and objectives of the school. All school charters include the National Education Guidelines which contain a statement of goals for New Zealand education, as well as curriculum and administrative requirements. Boards are required to consult with their local communities in setting up their charter. Boards of trustees are accountable for meeting the objectives of their charter and for managing the funds they receive from the government to run the school. They are required to present an annual report to their community and the Ministry of Education.

Students enrolling in a school agree to follow the policies and rules of the school. Boards may approve methods of discipline for students not in compliance such as withdrawal of privileges, setting extra homework or detentions. Suspension or expulsion follow more serious offenses.

School choice

Parents have the right to enroll their children in any state school of their choice, although if a school has too many children wishing to enroll, it has the right to limit enrollments to prevent overcrowding. School charters are available to assist parents in selecting schools for their children. In addition to their charter, each school is expected to have a prospectus or brochure that sets out its educational beliefs and what it intends to offer its students.

In addition to state schools for parents to choose from, integrated schools (previously private) receive the same per student funding as state schools, but building and land are privately owned so they meet the costs of property development and maintenance from attendance fees. They follow state curriculum but incorporate their own special character (philosophical or religious beliefs) in their program. Some state schools teach in the Maori language. Independent schools are governed by their own boards and receive a reduced level of state funding.

In spite of this choice policy, most children attend the school closest to where they live as "listed in the Yellow Pages of the telephone directory."

The New Zealand Curriculum Framework

Development of the national curriculum was prompted by a perceived need to raise standards of achievement and to change the nature and direction of what was being taught in the classroom to reflect changing needs of society. It was intended, as well, to help build a "seamless" education system. An apparently unprecedented initiative in New Zealand, the process of developing this curriculum has been unfolding over a number of years beginning in the early 90s. From time to time the process has been slowed in response to schools overwhelmed with changes. Support documents for the national curriculum are still in progress and plans have been announced to review the curriculum, as a whole, when current developments are complete.

The New Zealand Curriculum Framework is the foundation policy statement covering teaching, learning, and assessment for all students in all New Zealand schools. The framework addresses the following areas:
- identifies the principles on which all learning and teaching programs in New Zealand schools are to be based;

128

- identifies seven essential learning areas, each of which has a guideline prescribing the objectives to which each child should aim;
- defines eight groups of essential skills that students need to develop;
- outlines some of the attitudes and values that are an integral part of the curriculum, e.g., positive attitudes to learning and respect for others;
- sets out policies and procedures for assessment in all New Zealand schools, providing clear outcome statements against which students' progress can be measured.

The Ministry is accountable to teachers for providing the guidelines, resources and professional development to support curriculum implementation at least at the level of explanation. Schools and individual teachers are accountable to the Ministry and to parents and students for using the national curriculum framework and guidelines to develop school curricula and for planning classroom programs. Within each essential area the curriculum prescribes the student objectives that teachers are expected to use for their assessment plans and records of student progress. The level of accountability in these cases is explanation and possibly justification since schools and teachers need to convince students and parents that the program is relevant for them.

Board trustees are accountable to the Ministry for using the curriculum framework in the development of their school charter. Ultimately, all those responsible for the governance and operation of the school are accountable to students for providing them with an education that is responsive to their needs and abilities. As well, they are accountable to the larger community for developing citizens who are able and willing to contribute to the greater good of the community.

Education Review Office

The Education Review Office (ERO) is a government department reporting directly to the Minister and is charged with producing public reports on the quality of education in New Zealand schools and early childhood education centers. The ERO has about 100 review officers in its ten offices across the country and normally carries out an accountability review every three years for each school. It also publishes national reports on aspects of the overall education system.

In the context of the school reviews, the ERO is particularly interested in (a) what each board of trustees expects students to achieve and enjoy in their time at school and (b) how much the school knows about the actual learning of its students. To determine this, the school review process begins with notification of a date to begin the review, and requests such documentation from the school as its strategic plans, responses to a self-review questionnaire, and student achievement data. The school review also includes an on-site visit by ERO staff to talk to board members and professional staff, to read documents and to observe classes.

ERO reviewers eventually submit an "unconfirmed report" to the board and the board has up to 15 days to respond. Following this feedback, a "confirmed report" is prepared and sent to the board and the Ministry. This report contains recommendations and actions for the board, indicates when the school may be reviewed again, and includes a community summary page for easy communication to parents. These reports, and public documents available to any person on request, are intended to be a useful tool for the board of trustees and the principal for reviewing initiatives in any area of concern. The reports also are used by the Ministry to assess the support or assistance a school may need.

The school review process conducted by the ERO holds boards of trustees accountable for running their schools lawfully and for providing a good education for students. School staffs are accountable for the quality of teaching and learning. In both cases accountability is at the level of justification. Results of the school review process are available to parents to assist them in choosing schools for their children.

National examinations for secondary students

The New Zealand Qualifications Authority (NZQA), set up in 1990 to coordinate national qualifications, took over from several other agencies the responsibility to develop a national qualifications framework and to approve degrees. A Crown-owned agency headed by a board, (representing industry, community and education interests), the NZQA runs largely on a cost recovery basis. Apart from a government subsidy for the School Certificate, examinations are funded from candidates' fees. The government has now announced its policy (Achievement 2001) for the future of school qualifications. Achievement 2001 will see the National Certificate in Educational Achievement, levels 1–4 progressively replace all existing school awards 2001–2003. The NCEA will involve a balance of internal and external assessment in conventional school subjects. Sets of Achievement Standards will be developed for each subject and each standard will have credit value. The new standards will not be simply competency based, student performance will also be graded. A limited amount of credit may also be counted towards the NCEA from competency-based Unit Standards developed by non-government agencies such as Industry Training Organizations for non-conventional school subjects.

At the end of three years of secondary school (Year 11), most students take the School Certificate exam. Each candidate's course of study generally includes English, although the student is not required to sit the exam in that subject. A student may enter the examination in any number of subjects up to six and is credited with a grade from A to E in each subject.

After sixth form (Year 12), students receive the Sixth Form Certificate, awarded on a single-subject basis to students who have satisfactorily completed an approved course in one or more subjects. Grades are awarded on a 1 to 9 scale. A new policy for qualifications for 16–19 year olds is being developed for introduction from 2001. After Year 13 students are awarded a Higher School Certificate (perhaps for the last time in 1998) if they have satisfactorily completed five years of secondary schooling and have studied at least three subjects at a level about the Sixth Form Certificate. This certificate acknowledges course completion and does not have grades.

In Year 13 students take University Entrance, Bursary and Scholarship Examinations. Both percentage marks and grades are awarded. An A Bursary is awarded if total marks are 300 or higher, and B for marks ranging from 250 to 299. Grades also determine other awards. Entrance to university is achieved by gaining an A or B Bursary or by gaining

Higher School Certificate and three C grades or higher in the Bursary examination.

Changes to school qualifications are part of more general changes being made to the National Qualifications Framework. The NQF is a system for organizing, understanding, and relating qualifications. Qualifications are described in terms of their learning outcomes (the knowledge and skills a student would be expexted to have gained on completion of the qualification), level (the degree of complexity of the learning outcomes), and credit (signifying the amount of learning need to complete a qualification or component of a qualification).

These examination systems hold students accountable to their schools, parents and the wider public. Teachers also are indirectly accountable for ensuring their students have been prepared for the examinations. Although not stated explicitly, results of these examinations would probably be part of the school review process and would determine a school's public status on achievement. Consequences for the individual students include limits on their future education, training, and employment plans.

Assessment of primary students

In May of 1998 a Green Paper (Assessment for Success in Primary Schools) was issued for the purpose of obtaining feedback to a set of proposals aimed at improving assessment of primary students. According to this paper, primary (first eight years) students currently are assessed by their teachers using their own assessment tools, and some standardized assessment. But there are gaps in terms of externally referenced information that the proposed new assessment package is designed to address. Deadline for response to the proposals was August 7, 1998, with final decisions to be made by middle of 1999 to be announced in Government White Paper. By May 1999, the government still had not formally announced its policy.

A National Education Monitoring Project (NEMP) already samples primary student achievement at a national level to provide general indicators of how well the national curriculum is working. Nevertheless, the Green Paper claims that new tools are needed to remove perceived information gaps regarding the level of student achievement in primary grades.

The gaps to be filled are:
– diagnosis of specific learning needs or abilities;
– the standard a student should meet that indicates mastery of an achievement objective;
– how the achievement of students in a school compares with that of similarly aged students at a national level.

The proposed new package includes diagnostic tools in specific curriculum areas, and exemplars of student work referenced to the achievement objectives for all curriculum statements. The package also includes national tests referenced to the New Zealand Curriculum so that schools can analyze their students' achievement compared to national reference points, and modification of NEMP to provide more detailed information on achievement of specific groups of students.

These newly proposed initiatives hold students accountable for achieving standards set by the assessment policy. Teachers are accountable for providing a program consistent with the curriculum that will allow their students to achieve the standards. The level of accountability would probably be justification since outcomes are intended to be diagnostic as well as to provide information. Recipients of accounts and consequences are: (a) teachers who can use data for diagnosis of individual learning needs and program effectiveness, (b) parents who can compare individual and school achievement with national trends, (c) principals and boards who can identify the effectiveness of programs and provide additional information to their community, and (d) the government which can monitor the effectiveness of policy and formulate new policy.

Teacher Registration Board

The 1996 Education Amendment Act made registration compulsory for teachers, but also increased the responsibility of the Teacher Registration Board (TRB) to ensure that teachers continue to meet satisfactory teacher standards throughout their career. As of January 1, 1998 teachers are required to renew their practicing certificates every three years ($45 each time). This process is intended to be integrated with school's normal performance management and appraisal system that has been mandatory in schools since January 1, 1997. The TRB sends to each teacher the necessary document to be completed when the practice certificate comes due for renewal. A consultation procedure on standards for teachers (define a "satisfactory teacher") recently has been completed by the TRB.

Every three years teachers are able to renew their certificates if they are able to show that acceptable learning occurs for all students under their responsibility within an environment that affirms the bicultural and multicultural nature of New Zealand. A satisfactory teacher must demonstrate:

- knowledge of teaching and learning;
- good professional practice;
- relationships of trust, cooperation and respect for students, parents and colleagues;
- educational leadership relevant to the level of experience or responsibility being carried as a teacher or professional leader.

It is the responsibility of the school to give meaning to these generic dimensions and to specify skills, understandings, behaviors, and curriculum knowledge. The principal affirms in writing that the applicant is a satisfactory teacher and that he or she is engaged in professional development.

Teachers are accountable, at the level of justification, to the Teacher Registration Board. If they fail to meet the Board's standards they lose the right to teach.

School self-review

The requirement for schools to self review is stated in the Goverment's National Education Guidelines. School self-review is an internal review process that enables a school to evaluate how effectively it is meeting the goals it has adopted.

Self-review is intended to be a tool in helping schools provide the education parents want for their children. The government has also published guidelines including examples of school-based practice to help schools with the review process which is seen to be ongoing. The guidelines are flexible, granting considerable discretion to the board about how it carries out the review. The government also publishes a series of newsletters containing information and ideas about school review and development.

The review is considered most successful when it is carried out by a board of trustees, a principal, members of staff, and community representatives, all of whom have a shared vision and a commitment to effective change. The board is central to the process, either carrying out the review itself or organizing for it to be done. Self-review is part of any ongoing school renewal strategy that begins with review, resulting in planning, that leads to implementation, followed by monitoring, and ending in reporting before beginning the process again with self-review.

The whole school staff, or staff within particular programs, are being held accountable through this process, as is the board for how well it is managing the school. Accountability is at the level of justification and results of the school review and development process are reported in various ways to the those involved in the review, as well as to parents and the community at large. So the consequences should be a more effective school and a continual renewal of the school's mission. As well, the public should be more aware of how effectively the school is meeting its goals.

Interim professional standards for principals and teachers

Performance Management Systems (PMS) have been mandatory since January 1, 1997. The Ministry provided resource materials and training programs for boards, principals and teachers to develop skills in performance management and to integrate these systems in professional development strategies.

One way to enhance the PMS is to specify in more detail the important knowledge, skills, and attitudes that teachers and managers in schools need to perform their jobs well. In the spring of 1998, the government began a consultation process, ending in May of 1998, on a set of interim standards for school principals. A similar consultation is underway for deputy/assistant principals and primary teachers.

Performance standards describe the knowledge, skills and attitudes that all principals, deputies, or teachers are expected to demonstrate. The standards will form part of the performance management system of the school.

As part of the PMS, principals are required to have a performance agreement with their board that contains job descriptions professional standards, performance objectives, and development objectives. Boards will continue to be required to undertake an annual appraisal of the principal's performance but will, as of February 1999, carry out the appraisal against the professional standards. The interim principal standards are grouped into six key dimensions:
- professional leadership
- strategic management
- staff management
- relationship management
- financial and asset management
- statutory and reporting requirements.

A similar system is proposed for primary teachers and deputy/assistant principal with the principal being required to ensure that an annual appraisal of each teacher's and deputy/assistant principal's performance is carried out. It is expected that the professional standards will expand PMS so that they contain the following components:
- professional standards
- performance objectives/expectations
- development objectives.

The specific nature of these standards will emerge from a parallel review process related to teacher education and quality teaching underway at the time this paper was being written.

In the context of PMS, the principal is accountable to the board at the level of justification. Consequences for the principal include a directions for planning their own professional development, as well as changes in their remuneration. Teachers and deputies are accountable directly to the principal, but indirectly to the board of trustees which is their employer. The level of accountability is the same as for principals as are the consequences. In both cases, professional standards are expected to help teachers or principals and their boards identify the important knowledge, skills and attitudes required to be effective managers. The level of remuneration is planned to be tied to performance related to these standards.

School-level perspectives on accountability in New Zealand

This section describes the results of interviews with a small number of staff members, from a "convenience" sample of just two schools, about their understandings of accountability and their views of accountability initiatives in their country and school.

Nine school practitioners participated in the interviews. The head teachers at both the elementary and senior schools were interviewed. Five elementary and two secondary teachers also participated.

Question 1: How do you understand the term accountability in the context of your own school and classroom?

Participants, speaking about their understanding and interpretation of the term accountability, focused their comments on the people and groups to whom they felt responsible. 90 percent of teachers' and administrators' referred to their students when asked to describe their thoughts on accountability. Their comments frequently addressed their sense of personal responsibility for student learning and development. Many senior level teachers also highlighted their role in ensuring that students mastered and performed well on the national standardized tests. Parents of current students were mentioned within both teachers' and administrators' discussions of their perceptions of accountability. Half of the sample felt that parents needed to be aware of the school activities and student progress.

More than two thirds of teachers and administrators express a sense of responsibility to the government, its educational branches and the national curriculum. Only secondary teachers mentioned their duty to implement curriculum, however. In each case, teachers discussed essential skill assessment, classroom evaluation or national testing.

Three teachers mentioned their sense of responsibility to their communities, society and future employers. Teachers also expressed their personal sense of responsibility towards their schools, their professional development and their employers. One teacher also explained her sense of responsibility to be able to clearly outline her actions and work.

"We are responsible for what we do. We are held responsible for what we do and what is done within the school. Whatever you do you have to be sure you can back it up. You have to be careful."

Question 2: Who are your clients? Who are the other stakeholders? What are their needs and wants?

Students, parents and the community were the most frequently mentioned client and stakeholder groups. While students and parents were mentioned by all participants, the community was mentioned by 80 percent of participants. School-level administrators were also highlighted as a key interest group.

Every teacher and administrator interviewed isolated students as the school and school system's primary client group. Interviewees shared an overall commitment to the schools' role in preparing students for their future lives. Several teachers also mentioned their desire to assist all students in developing an understanding of their personal role in their education and its impact on their lives.

Everyone interviewed agreed that parents were also the school's primary client group. Teachers expressed differing opinions about parental needs and the degree of accountability they both demand and should be given. Four participants felt that parents had a broad range of interests in the school and their children's school life. Along these lines, one teacher commented that on parental needs:

138

"They want kids to be happy and feel safe here. They want an environment where there is no bullying, where classes run well and there are lots of opportunities. We are now beginning to advertise the school's success and promote these things."

Teachers also discussed the importance of having tools that provide tangible evidence of student achievement, both individually and against the national curriculum and outcomes. Report cards and teacher-parent interview sessions were highlighted as the most frequent means of communicating with parents.

Many teachers and administrators discussed parental accountability in terms of communication. The creation of methods for drawing parents into the schools and making parents aware of student achievement were important at both schools. Newsletters, career and sporting evenings were mentioned. The elementary-level participants also remarked on their attempts to consult their constituencies. One school had surveyed parents, staff and students to determine each group's vision of the school. The results of the survey assisted the school in developing its mission statement.

Teachers felt that school-level administrators and managers were responsible for demanding and ensuring accountability of teachers and students. For example:

"The Head of Department, checks learning outcomes and monitors them. You are pulled all over to show what you have done. You are held accountable.
There are Deans for each year [grade]. They make all the contact with parents.
The Head of House also ensures accountability. They monitor attendance. They have a really rigorous system, monitored period by period making it hard to be absent."

Ninety percent of participants identified the general community as a major stakeholder and client group within the schools. The greater society, future employers, caregivers and other community agencies were cited as essential clients of the school.

Administrators and administrative branches of government featured prominently in many teacher's discussions of clients and stakeholders. Several teachers and administrators felt accountable to the school board. For example:

"I feel more accountable to the board than the government because the board is responsible to the government. It's a hierarchy thing. The school is shaped by the board. In turn, the board should reflect the community. They should and they do want it to be a happy, successful school."

Many of the secondary teachers isolated the government as a major stakeholder in the education process although none of the elementary teachers did. Those who did discussed the government in terms of their role in ensuring teachers and schools were being held accountable for their teaching. Their comments often related to the government's lack of frequent communication with teachers and schools. Current funding decisions, curriculum guidelines and attendance registers were noted as other government-based accountability initiatives. One teacher added:

"The government is certainly a stakeholder because they pay your wage and they set the overall policies."

Question 3: What do you do at the present time that might be considered accountability?

When asked to comment on their current accountability-driven practices, teachers and administrators concentrated on several issues. Teacher appraisal processes, student level achievement measures, parental and administrative reporting mechanisms were highlighted by participants.

The teacher appraisal process was frequently mentioned by participants as a means for addressing accountability. Participants commented on the formative process of teacher appraisal, which included collaborative peer-based professional development efforts, and the annual summative appraisal system. As one teacher explained:

140

"Once a year, each teacher and the head of department meet. This evaluation is then passed on to the principal. This is an opportunity to show that there is constant improvement and provide incentive. Classroom visits are also used. In addition, the criteria used to determine teaching competencies are taken from the national employment contracts."

Many of the teachers supported the appraisal program and highlighted the value of the program's checklists and personal records. The flexibility the government offered the schools, in terms of professional development, was seen in a positive light by both teachers and administrators. In terms of the peer assessment and professional development work, one teacher positively responded to the fact that they can select their own assessor.

Student achievement records were mentioned by six participants as a common accountability tool. Benchmarking student work at different times of the year was also seen as a positive evaluation practice. Two teachers also described the move toward curriculum surveys that measure individual school curriculum against the national standards.

All participants mentioned the role of parent/teacher and parent/teacher/student meetings as a way to promote greater accountability and communication. The role of the Head of the Department, in terms of budget preparation, staff development and orientation, classroom observation and dealing with behavior incidents, was described as a measure of bureaucratic accountability. Teachers and administrators also noted the increased role of the board of trustees in ensuring school-level accountability. One teacher explained:

"Schools file their reports to the Board of Trustees (BOT) and give signs to alert them of possible resources problems. Projects, long-term and mid-term goals, and past reviews are also BOT responsibility."

Question 4: As there is no district school-level in New Zealand this question has not been asked.

Question 5: What initiatives from the government-level can you identify that seem to be aimed at increasing accountability?

In response to this question, participants identified seven different nationally driven accountability initiatives. Public accountability was one of these initiatives. Several teachers mentioned the media's impact on school-level accountability efforts. Both administrators expressed concern with the publication of school results and its potentially negative impact on the schools. One teacher expressed these sentiments:

> "The publishing of school and exam results, often with little thought given to what decile (socioeconomic level) the school is at, makes schools more aware of their accountability."

Teacher evaluation and assessment practices were highlighted by many participants as one of the government's major accountability initiatives. The new appraisal system was mentioned by several teachers. For example, two teachers outlined the system and highlighted its role in teacher professional development. As part of the appraisal system, each teacher has a peer appraiser. You are accountable to improve yourself and to set goals.

> "Appraisal for all staff is development-oriented. Its goal is to take them from where they are, valuing what they do, but also giving them a path for professional development.
> Each staff has their own professional development budget which they administer themselves.
> The job description is huge, cut and dry, and makes you look like you have to be the perfect teacher. In some ways it is too much."

Several teachers expressed their concern with the negative impact of the teacher appraisal program and the extra effort it requires:

> "I don't think the government realizes how much time it takes up. It can be disastrous. It can be detrimental.
> Workload issues, class sizes, can make it [appraisal and professional

development] harder. We are getting less time to do the job [of teaching] and its making the job less attractive."

Teachers had mixed reactions towards student evaluation initiatives. Several secondary teachers commented on the impact of 'unit standards' on the teacher and their classroom activities. For example:

"More reporting systems make it seem like quality checked education in effect is actually removing a lot of the quality in our education system. If your whole time is consumed by assessments, then a lot of learning is directed at that assessment task. That doesn't make you a better teacher.
Stress is being placed on schools with the introduction of unit standards while other forms of assessment are still in place, e. g., external exams. Unit standards have lost direction and have resulted in double assessment and double marking."

Other teachers discussed their practices and processes of conducting individual student assessment. They commented on the student portfolio that records all work completed and attempted by each student.

Increasingly, schools are being required to provide accounts for their actions. One teacher discussed the current move toward school-level accountability:

"Setting up the quality management systems, the accreditation document made schools aware that things had to be written down, everything had to be documented. This has had a positive effect, even if it is time-consuming."

When discussing school-level accountability issues, several teachers spoke of the practice of school/school comparisons. One teacher remarked on the reliability of inter-school comparisons:

"Comparing school with school is not really an indication of how well you are doing because of [the impact] of your decile rating."

Half of the participants mentioned funding as a government tool to increase accountability. Neither of the administrators did so, however. All funding comments were focused on the bulk funding of teacher salaries. Teachers explained, for example:

> "Bulk funding, the direct resourcing issue, is floating around and hasn't gone away. Seen as a way of making teachers more accountable to their own local community, the idea is that people will vote with their feet. But, they do that anyway.
> We are given a certain amount of money depending on the student numbers. Schools are then responsible for putting money into the places they need it. So if schools run out of money, they are in trouble. It is very pleasing for the government to have bulk funded schools. There are very few of them so they get wonderful reports. But at some schools, 60 teachers have left in two years. Bulk funding doesn't do much for stability."

One administrator added his/her thoughts on the bulk funding issue:

> "Bulk-funding schools bring in the issue of employing younger and cheaper staff. This is supposed to happen in the bulk-funded schools. It is important though to show that you are not employing younger staff."

An elementary teacher explained his/her perception of the Pay Parity campaign, to level the remuneration of elementary and secondary teachers.

> "A school can now award points to people who are seen to be doing particularly well in an area. We are in the process of trying to decide who to give the points to. It is causing dissent."

Three-quarters of participants mentioned the Education Review Office (ERO) as a mechanism to make schools more accountable. Teachers explained the role of the ERO and the impact of their school-level assessment practices.

"Staff feel under pressure anytime an ERO visit is announced. Old inspectors used to look at the individual teachers but the ERO looks at the whole school.

Some guidelines and expectation are far-fetched. There isn't enough time, it's stretching the limit. So many decisions about education are made without consulting the teachers. Quality control has to be realized but we can't expect to do what is not humanly possible.

Their time pressure is so great. They are coming in and having to do a quick one-off look at something, making a statement and then leaving. They are playing less of a developmental role."

With respect to the "Green Paper on Assessment," teachers at the elementary level expressed their frustration with the way government policies are introduced. Their concern was primarily focused at the proposed changes in student assessment practices and the potential introduction of a national testing program. For example:

"Pamphlets showed up at the schools outlining suggestions for national testing. No previous information had been given to teachers. These pamphlets were to be distributed to the parents.

National initiatives influence what goes on in the schools, we want to have lots of emphasis on developing effective teachers and we certainly don't want to have to narrow our focus because of what is being implemented at the national level."

Teacher concern for their students was evident. Speaking on the prospect of national testing, one teacher added:

"The idea is measuring children against other children in other areas. I don't see how that is going to work. Every school has different needs and the children [at each school] are completely different."

Hungary

Background

The political and economic changes that have evolved since the early 1990s have effected all aspects of Hungarian social policy. Within the context of these changes, the education system has become committed to its goal to develop and strengthen the democratic principles it adheres to. In 1996, after much discussion and debate, the government unveiled its framework for the future of the Hungarian education system. The paper, entitled "The Strategy of the Long-Term Development Hungarian Public Education" addresses the issues of the role of education within society, the education system and its management and financing. This paper also served to support the national emphasis placed on expanding secondary and tertiary educational opportunities.

Although the federal Ministry of Culture and Education is responsible for guiding the education system, several other ministries and levels of government play an active role in education policy and decision-making. Local governments are given the task of providing primary and secondary level educational opportunities for children within their boundaries. Local authorities are also responsible for budgets, administrative appointments, curricular and pedagogical approaches and the establishment of school rules and plans.

Traditionally, the Hungarian education system had been centralized and regulated. Within the last decade, there has been a devolution of authority as schools and local governments have gained a greater level of autonomy. The mandatory application of central plans has been discontinued in favor of local initiatives. Teaching and learning initiatives have also been downloaded to the local level.

While children are required to attend school beginning at age six, most children attend preschool between the ages of three and six. From age six to 14, children attend a general school. Upon completion, students attend one of three secondary schools depending on their skills and past academic achievements. Students' secondary school opportunities include: Gimnazium, a four-year general academic school; Szak-

146

kozepiskola, a four-year vocational school; or, Szakmunkaskepzo, a three-year vocational training school.

Accountability policies in Hungary

The Education Act

The Education Act (1993, 1996) established the framework for the Hungarian education system. Within the Act, local governments are made responsible for maintaining schools in their district. Financial assistance from the national level is also made available.

The Act outlines the requirements and framework of compulsory education in Hungary. Children are required to attend school for a total of ten years between ages six and 16. Although all students are required to attend school during this period, there are several options at the secondary school-level. Students may attend either an academic or vocationally-oriented school. If Students leave school upon completion of their ten-year commitment, they are required to complete a leaving examination.

Amendments to the Education Act

In 1996, there were a series of amendments made to the Education Act. The principle goal of the changes was the decentralization of educational authority and decision-making power. Several implications of the amendments included: the decreased legal opportunity for state level intervention; the empowerment of the teaching profession; and, more autonomy for the local level educational participants. The new National Core Curriculum (NCC) was also launched within the context of the amendments. In addition, the duration of compulsory schooling was increased from eight to ten years. This supported the education system's goal of creating a more educated population and increasing the number of students eligible for higher education programs.

Compulsory teacher training and more developed career development program were also introduced. Funding structures were also revamped. This change resulted in the development funding mechanisms that allocates an annual sum within the schools and school systems.

Governance and school boards

In 1990, school ownership was transferred from the state to local level governments. The Law of Self-Governance resulted in the state becoming responsible for the maintenance of schools. In some cases, ownership of the school may be shared with the local community, churches, etc. In effect, any legally eligible person or group may be eligible to establish a school. Each local government and school elects a school board. Each board serves an advisory capacity and assists schools in their decision-making processes. In most cases, they are composed of community members, parents and school-level staff.

Secondary school curriculum and structure

In 1989, In support of the national emphasis on creating a stronger secondary education system, a series of curricular and structural changes were adopted. In the past, secondary schools had provided students with a four-year curriculum. Currently, secondary school programs are offered for four, six, or eight years. Students may be admitted to secondary school upon their completion of four, six, or eight years of primary school. The duration of primary school is dependent on the nature of the level of specialization offered. Vocational secondary schools are often six years in length and offer students the opportunity to receive specialized training.

In 1995, the new National Core Curriculum (NCC) was approved for implementation during the 1998/1999 school year. The democratic foundation of the NCC objectives are inspired by the need for all students to have to opportunity to learn and adopt democratic values. The objectives of the NCC are to address and respect basic human rights, freedom of choice and minority rights. Accordingly, all schools offering programs from grades 1 to 10 must adhere to the guidelines and foundations set forth in the NCC. It is hoped that this unity will enable students to move more freely within the system and between schools.

The NCC delegates authority to the local governments and individual schools to design and enhance curriculum in order to meet the needs of its population. Within the text of the NCC, participants and stakeholders are encouraged to participate in curricular and school program development. For example, the NCC allows parents, students and school leaders to express their interests and values, promotes professional ambitions of teachers and allows the consideration of prevailing conditions, circumstances and opportunities.

In order for schools and teachers to be able to achieve the goals outlined within the NCC, while maintaining their ability to cater to the needs of their respective populations, the following guidelines were adopted:

– The objectives outlined in the NCC, can be achieved in 50–70 percent of the time allocated to each level of achievement. Thus, the NCC allows the introduction of supplementary contents and objectives.
– It formulates contents and objectives according to comprehensive culture domains instead of teaching subjects, enabling schools to choose, establish and group their teaching subject individually.
– It does not determine objectives for each grade, but lays down stages and objectives to be met by the time students finish certain grades (i.e. 4, 6, 8, 10).

The NCC isolates ten cultural domains within which the curriculum is to be taught. They are as follows: mother tongue and literature, modern foreign language, mathematics, man and society, man and nature, our earth and environment, arts, informatics, life management and practical studies, physical education and sports.

Within each of the aforementioned categories, the NCC outlines attainment targets for students in grades 4, 6, 8, and 10. The targets are comprised of knowledge, skills, and minimum competency requirements. In addition, cross-curricular objectives are highlighted throughout the document and link school-wide educational activities. The cross-curricular objectives include: homeland, integration into Europe, integration into the world environmental education, communication culture, physical and mental education, learning, and career orientation.

Within the text of the NCC, the Ministry of Culture and Education asserts its responsibility for providing both in-service training and support for teachers.

Minority language teaching

The NCC outlines the curricular objectives aimed at the education of national and ethnic minorities. Language and cultural traditions are highlighted as key areas of curriculum within which students can develop an appreciation of their heritage and that of their fellow students. Within the NCC, any of Hungary's 13 minority languages may be taught as a foreign language or as a language of education. The choice of language rests with the schools.

Student assessment

In accordance with the new National Core Curriculum, there has been serious discussion of the potential of a national testing procedure for students. The development of an examination system will add specificity to the process of evaluating and assessing student achievement. There is also discussion of the Ministry of Culture and Education's role in the development of a comprehensive and compatible student evaluation system.

In most states, school reporting consists of an evaluation at the end

150

of each of two terms. While a traditional report card is issued at the end of the first term, a certificate of achievement is issued upon completion. Student achievement is traditionally graded on a five-point scale. For example: 5 (excellent), 2 (pass) and 1 (fail). In many cases, students attaining a failing grade may sit a supplementary exam in order to progress to the next grade.

Students do not write standardized examinations upon completion of primary school. Admission to secondary school is dependent on their previous academic achievement. This, in combination with a student's interests and abilities, determines their eligibility for academic or vocationally-based schools.

Upon completion of secondary school, students may elect to participate in a final or maturity examination. Students attending academic secondary institutions, may elect to take the maturity examination. These students are then examined by a board of external examiners. Current discussions indicate the pending implementation of a compulsory examination upon completion of basic education in grade 10; and, a secondary final exam in grade 12.

In addition, students interested in attending university must sit university set exams and met their determined standards.

Teacher training and professionalization

Teachers are expected to adhere to the tenants expressed in the Hungarian Constitution, the Declaration of Human Rights, and the Charter for Children. Professional development occurs both within the school and from the local level.

Teacher training in Hungary consists of a tiered and clearly divided system. While kindergarten teachers are required to complete a three-year college program, lower primary teachers participate in a three or four-year schoolmasters college program. Upper primary teachers must complete a four year primary school teachers diploma. Secondary general education teachers participate in traditional university programs and receive a school teachers diploma in five years.

Teacher training faculties of universities specializing in the vocational subjects including agriculture and economics serve as the training ground for secondary vocational teachers. Special education teachers must complete their teachers diploma from a teacher training college.

In 1992, the Law of Public Employees acknowledged the teaching profession as a member of the public service. In turn, employees of schools are paid within the standard governmental pay-scale and were introduced to more stringent employment regulations.

In terms of teacher development, both the NCC and the Education Act Amendments introduced the subject of more developed professional development activities and strategies.

System evaluation

The use of educational research in Hungarian educational policy development has been a tradition. The center for evaluation studies of the institute of public education supports the collection and dissemination of assessment data and evaluation tools. Current research interests and priorities include teacher training, teaching and learning processes, educational structures and financing strategies.

School-level perspectives on accountability in Hungary

This section describes the results of interviews with a small number of staff members, from a "convenience" sample of just two schools, about the their understandings of accountability and their views of accountability initiatives in their country and school.

Eight school practitioners participated in the interview process. At the senior level school, the headmaster and four teachers were interviewed. The elementary school headmaster and three teachers also participated.

Question 1: How do you understand the term accountability
in the context of your own school and classroom?

Interviewees discussed their desire to encourage the autonomy of their
pupils. Teachers also expressed their sense of duty towards the "rules of
the school." For clarification, one teacher described the "rules of the
school" as a school-driven plan that outlines student and teacher conduct standards. They also mentioned strategic planning-oriented activities.

Many teachers and administrators discussed the role of the "rules of
the school," and the importance of relationships between teachers and
pupils. One teacher also commented on the head master's role in setting direction for the school.

One-third of the participants discussed the government's role in
creating and implementing accountability-driven initiatives. Both the
Government Act and the Public Education Act were isolated as key
legislation in the government's plan to increase educational accountability. Teachers and administrators outlined the three accountability-
based elements of the legislation. According to participants, these
documents set out guidelines for the school's material responsibility,
behavioral responsibility, and duty to ensure the safety of students.

Question 2: Who are your clients? Who are other relevant stakeholders?
What are some examples of their needs and wants?

Students were unanimously cited by all participants as important
clients in the educational process. Eighty-five percent of participants
also listed teachers as clients. By comparison, parents were mentioned
by 77 percent of participants. The headmaster, the school management
and the police were also acknowledged as key clients of the school and
school system.

Outside organizations, including those relating to student hobbies,
were named as stakeholders by all but one secondary school participant. One-third of participants highlighted the "community of bour-
geois" as another important stakeholder. The "foundation of the

school," an association that helps and aids the poor pupils, was also recognized. Again, the police, teachers, students and parents were mentioned.

All of the participants were cognizant of their role in meeting student needs. These needs included the attainment of greater levels of knowledge, participating in interesting lessons and direct contact with teachers. Again, the relationship between students and teachers was noted as an important and integral part of the educational experience. Parental need, as defined by the interview participants, concentrated on their students successful completion of the university-qualifying exams, development of a knowledge of languages, and information science. Several participants remarked on the relationship between the rules of the school and the school-level administration. It appeared that most participants felt that there was a lack of authority vested in the role of the school-level administrator or headmaster. One participant noted:

"Headmaster's jurisdiction is missing from the public education act. For this reason ... there is a need to enlarge the school autonomy."

Another teacher commented on the school's responsibility for creating liaisons and cooperating with parents, pupils and the government. One teacher commented that in many ways, "the school has become the second family."

Participants also commented on governmental needs and wants and focused on the government programming. Within these discussions, participants mentioned the Public Education Act, the National Curriculum and the UNESCO children's chart as the primary elements of government interest. Another teacher noted school competition as directed by the school district.

Question 3: What do you at the present time that might be considered accountability according to this definition?

Most teachers identified their efforts to address student behavior problems as an example of their accountability-driven activities. Two-thirds

154

of teachers touched on the line of authority and process by which they contend with behavior issues. These steps included a verbal warning, conversations with the student, discussions with parents and finally the headmaster. Communication with parents and the headmaster, in addition to tracking student absenteeism, were also noted as accountability initiatives.

One-third of participants referred to the "rules of teacher," a part of the "rules of school" and the code of ethics as measures to increase accountability. Several teachers also referred to the JOB ACT, as a means for dealing with any problems with the teachers.

Question 4: What initiatives from the school district-level can you identify that seem to be aimed at increasing accountability?

Secondary participants, and one of their elementary colleagues, addressed the role of the teacher in developing relationships with their students. Establishing "daily connections with pupils" and promoting "open connectiveness between the teachers and the pupils" was mentioned by several teachers. The teachers "rules of the school" and their responsibility towards their colleagues were mentioned by two teachers. Again, participants mentioned the government's need to increase the autonomy and control assigned to the headmaster. Two teachers also discussed the daily contact the headmaster has with students.

Three participants highlighted the "creation of new school rules" and the role of the school in clarifying these rules as examples of current accountability initiatives. One teacher explained their annual school conference:

"Once a year at the school conference, problems come up for discussion and stimulate school democracy."

Question 5: What initiatives from the government-level can you identify that seem to be aimed at increasing accountability?

Three government initiatives were identified by participants. One of these was the Public Education Act. Participants commented on their perceptions of government accountability. One quarter of participants mentioned that they felt the Public Education Act decreased the practice of accountability. Half of the participants were of the opinion that students were protected from teachers by the Act and by other government initiatives.

One teacher felt that there was no connection between the education policy and school practice. And several teachers agreed with their colleague that "The headmasters duty is being limited by the Public Education Act. It has a negative influence on education."

Half of the participants discussed the government's practice of frequently referring to the UNESCO child chart. In discussing government initiatives, one participant noted:

"In my opinion, there is chaos because there are too many government acts and too little emphasis placed on the school business federation."

It is interesting to note that half of those interviewed did not or could not identify national accountability initiatives. And two-thirds felt that national initiatives had no influence on educational practice in the schools.

Germany

Background

The Federal Republic of Germany is comprised of 16 Länder. The Unification Treaty (1990) resulted in the creation of five new Länder and served as the catalyst for the establishment of five new Ministries of Education and Cultural Affairs and Science. The Standing Conference of the Ministers of Education and Cultural Affairs (1990) created a common educational framework and initiated a more cooperative liaison between the Länder and the federal government. The Conference also stimulated a reorganization of the school system.

The German school system is a state system with the Ministry of Education and Cultural Affairs of the respective "Land" being the highest educational authority. The Ministry sets guidelines of education and determines the curricula. Thus the Land provides a framework that ensures continuity and allows for standardized methods of student evaluation.

The Länder are solely responsible for the administration of education policy. Within this context, the Länder are also responsible for the following: organizing school structures; developing course content; creating teaching objectives; supervising teacher work; and, textbook approval and selection.

Children are required to attend school from age six, for nine or ten years. Following this period, students are required to enroll in either full-time upper secondary general education or vocational school. Attendance records are taken seriously and truancy can result in actions against students and/or parents.

Accountability policies in Germany

Education governance

Each Land is represented at the Bundesrat, the representative seat of government. Within the Bundesrat, the Cultural Affairs Committee, the Internal Affairs Committee and the Committee for Issues of the European Union share responsibility for the development of education and science policy.

Within most Länder, there are three levels of educational governance. The upper level consists of the Ministry of Education and Cultural Affairs. The lower levels are comprised of the regional school department, with authority over the Gymnasium and Realschule, and the local government's school offices that oversee the Grundschulen,

Hauptschulen und Sonderschulen. The Länder share joint responsibility with the regional authorities for education.

School system

Local youth welfare agencies are responsible for administering preschool-level educational programs. Both the Kindergarten, an institution offering preschool programs for three to five year-olds, and the Schulkindergarten, for six year-old students who are not ready to attend school, are accountable to educational authorities.

Primary schools (Grundschule) covers grades 1 to 4 (ages six to ten). In two Länder, Berlin and Brandenburg, Grundschule continues until grade 6 (age 12). Usually students remain with the same teacher for the first two years, after which subject-based teachers cooperate with the class teacher.

Secondary school

Most children attend secondary school from the ages of ten to 16. Within most schools, the initial two years serve as an orientation period for students. After completing the lower secondary school grade, students move on to either an academic or vocational upper secondary schools. Student ability and desire, parental consultation, and school-level evaluations are all considered when deciding which upper secondary route students will take. Although in most cases the final decision rests with the parents, there are certain schools that will only admit students based on their performance or school endorsement. Students commence their upper secondary school studies after they have completed their compulsory education, approximately age 15.

Leaving certificates are issued upon successful completion of a given level of education. Certificates, issued by the Ministry, are signed by the head and classroom teachers. To ensure the sanctity of the upper secondary school-leaving certificate the Standing Conference coordinates discussions and decisions among the school authorities of the Länder.

School-level participation

The Education Act and school laws often provide opportunities for members of the educational process to participate. Through a variety of councils, parents, teachers, students and other stakeholders participate in the decision-making process.

The Teacher's Council is composed of all the teachers in a school. Its responsibilities cover both the discussion of professional and educational matters of the school and the decision on organizational matters in general. Decisions which the different departments are concerned with (e. g., school books for the specific subject) are prepared in the Department Council (Fachkonferenz). Here the parents and students are represented.

The School Council is designed to increase participation in school decision-making processes and encourage cooperation between teachers, pupils, parents and head teachers. Each Land determines the relative composition of each constituency and the degree of authority vested in the Council. These councils are responsible for student safety issues, school rules, scheduling, extracurricular activities and course content. Most councils have the authority to make decisions affecting homework supervision, and pilot project participation. In selected Länder, Councils play a role in selecting head teachers.

Student Councils are important vehicles for student participation. Students elect representatives from their peer groups at their class or grade level. This Council elects a school level representative that will represent their personal interests at the district or Länder level student forum. It is expected that students will have the opportunity to hold relevant meetings and discussions.

Parents have the opportunity to participate at various levels. Although each Land is different, many Länder encourage parental participation at both the classroom and the school level. In some cases, parent councils are also convened at the regional and Länder level.

School choice

Primary school students must attend their local school. At the secondary level, parents may make an application for their children to attend a school outside their local jurisdiction. School authorities can make the final decision on the student's acceptance to the schools.

As far as their choice of the type of secondary school is concerned, parents are given advice by the primary school.

Funding

Ninety percent of educational funding is provided by Länder and local educational authorities. In most cases, the Länder and the local authorities provide 20 percent and 80 percent of school expenses. Preschool education is not sponsored by the aforementioned authorities but is left in the hands of other government agencies. Parents are required to pay a portion of the costs. The level of their payment is relative to their salary, and they have the opportunity to apply for full or partial funding.

Curriculum reform

The Ministry of Education and Cultural Affairs is responsible for the development of school curriculum. Although teachers are permitted to personalize their choice of instructional techniques, groups of teachers who are assigned to the same curricular material often work together to design a comprehensive and consistent educational approach.

Curriculum reform, often taking months or years, is coordinated by the Ministry. The curriculum committee is traditionally comprised of current teachers, head teachers, school inspectors, members of the Länder's school research institute and, occasionally, academics.

New curriculum is often pilot-tested and reviewed by parental and student associations. Upon the acceptance of the new curriculum, the teacher associations provide the appropriate in-service training programs and textbook publishers work to create the appropriate texts.

Student evaluation

Students in grades 1 and 2 participate in observation-based evaluation practices. Reports on student progress are issued annually and detail student strengths and weaknesses. More traditional written tests are introduced in grade 3 in conjunction with the use of bi-annual numerical reports. Student achievement is compared with that of their peers and is used to determine students' educational future.

While students in grade 1 automatically progress to the next level, students in grades 2, 3 and 4 must be granted permission to progress. Upon completion of primary school, the vote of the school is used to determine the student's eligibility for secondary school. Each Land has different regulations on the power invested in the school vote as an arbiter of student progression.

Secondary level evaluation is based on written, oral and practical student work. Grades are distributed along a six-point scale with 1 = very good and 6 = very poor. Reports are issued bi-annually and may reflect a student's academic, social and behavioral performance. Standardized tests administered at the Land level are only conducted in individual Länder. If there are indications that a student will not be eligible to progress to the next grade, teachers are responsible for notifying parents during the mid-term report.

Teacher evaluation

Until recently, the main measures taken to ensure high quality of teaching in Germany have consisted in so-called "input control," i.e., by improving teacher education and training (at the university level, during training and by continuous education throughout the teacher's career). As well, the Ministry provides the teachers with information and advice. In addition, teachers are evaluated by inspectors who are under the authority of the Ministry. Other measures are concerned with the distribution of human and financial resources, which is highly centralized. Teachers, for instance, are assigned to schools by the Ministry.

161

Educational reform

The current motivation for changing the system is in large part economical. Globalization has given rise to the fear that students may not be getting the foundation they need to be competitive in the international markets. The difficult economic situation of many European countries in general and some German states in particular has also created a pressure to develop more efficient and effective schools and to demand greater responsibility in the use of financial resources.

The present discussion of educational policy in Germany focuses mainly on quality assurance and evaluation. New policies concerning quality assurance and evaluation have already been implemented in a number of Länder. In some of those the policies are still on an experimental level.

Two trends in quality assurance

Recent changes in education policy have focused on quality assurance. In the words of the education minister of North Rhine-Westfalia, Gabriele Behler, "quality assurance in schools is nowadays on everyone's lips." The initiative to change education policy has to come from the Ministry of Education and Cultural Affairs in each Land. Some German Länder have already made or prepared changes in education policies in order to enhance quality assurance.

Two main trends can be identified with regard to recent reforms and initiatives directed at the primary and secondary school system in various Länder.

One trend is towards reforming the system from within, strengthening and modernizing the existing administrative structure. This is to be achieved through improved transparency, deregulation, enhancing management qualities of school administrators and to some extent increased administrative responsibility given to the schools. While advisory functions of the school boards are improved, they still maintain their double function of supervising and advising, an arrangement which is now heavily debated. This trend leaves the hierarchical structure of the bureaucratic system intact. This approach is prominent in the Länder of Bavaria and Baden-Württemberg. Saxony can also be mentioned in this context. At the beginning of 1999 its school supervisory board was restructured, however, which resulted in one hierarchical lebel being dropped.

A second trend can be found in the states North Rhine-Westfalia, Bremen and Hessen. The goal there is to bring about changes in the administrative structure by decentralization as well as by emphasizing the autonomy and responsibility of the individual schools. Within the framework of the general curriculum prescribed by the Ministry, schools are required to define their goals and priorities in a school program. They must also submit themselves to internal and external evaluations. We will refer to this second trend as the New Model for quality assurance.

A New Model for quality assurance and evaluation

The main feature of the New Model is a replacement of the system of central state authority with a decentralized system which gives autonomy and responsibility to the schools. This movement towards school autonomy has pedagogical and political reasons. It is hoped that greater school autonomy will increase teachers' engagement and motivation. The implementation of the New Model often goes hand in hand with cutbacks in government funding for education. The assumption is that greater autonomy leads to increased financial responsibility of the schools, encouraging them to cut spending and seek private funding for special projects.

The New Model requires new methods for monitoring school quality. Here some hard questions come up: "How does one measure the quality of a school?," "What is a good school?." According to the New Model, there is no single standard to measure the quality of schools. Each school must set out its goals and priorities in a school program, which then serves as the standard of quality for that school. The school is to initiate a democratic process involving all parties concerned in order to form and revise the school program. The proponents of the

New Model tend to reject centralized methods of ranking or comparing school performance, because it neglects the different backgrounds and individuality of the schools.

This model requires the schools to evaluate their performance according to the standards laid out in the school program. School evaluations are primarily internal (self-evaluations), in some cases they are followed by external evaluations. The evaluation process, and the role of the school boards, will be considered in our discussion of recent policy changes in individual states.

North Rhine-Westfalia

In 1992, North Rhine-Westfalia introduced a model project named "School Development and School Supervision, Quality Development and Quality Assurance of Schools." QUESS focused on quality assurance and evaluation. The project was experimental and its results have barely been integrated into educational policy in North Rhine-Westfalia. It does, however, point the way to changes in educational policy that are now beginning to take place.

The central idea of QUESS is the decentralization of the school system by giving more autonomy to single schools. It tries to transform schools into "houses of learning" as education minister Gabriele Behler puts it. QUESS focuses on internal and external evaluation as means to quality assurance, but the introduction and development of school programs as well as the role of the school boards are also prominent parts of the project.

The main goals are:
– Education and support for schools and school boards in further developing and improving the quality of educational work.
– Clarification of the tasks and roles of the school boards in giving support and advice for school development processes.
– Development and testing of methods for school evaluation and quality assurance.
– Development and testing of methods for school boards in external evaluations and quality assurance.

164

The main results of the project are:
- Schools should be responsible for the process and method of evaluation.
- Evaluation should be embedded in a development process.
- Participation of school boards in evaluation can be critical.
- Schools need accessible instruments for evaluation.
- Schools need external support and training for evaluation.

The project was initiated in 1992 and was concluded in 1997. Nineteen schools participated in the project. They developed individual school programs, which, nonetheless, had to be within the existing curricula outlined by the Ministry. Students and parents were involved in the development of the school programs. The schools were responsible for self-evaluations, followed by external evaluations conducted by the school boards, taking the self-evaluations into account. Within QUESS, the school boards maintained their double function of supervising and providing advice and support to the schools.

Experimental projects, such as QUESS, may meet with enthusiasm within the schools and school boards involved, but general, structural changes to the education system are not expected to be implemented without some resistance and conflict.

The same year QUESS was introduced, a special Committee on Education (Bildungskommission) was established by the Prime Minister of North Rhine-Westfalia. It completed its report in 1995. The report made a number of recommendations that are related to quality assurance in schools, in particular with regard to school autonomy, school programs and self-evaluations.

QUESS and the Report of the Committee on Education serve as the basis for changes in education policy now taking place in North Rhine-Westfalia. One important difference between the QUESS project and the Report consists in their suggestions for the role of the school board. While QUESS suggests that the school board keep its double function of advising and supervising the schools, the Committee on Education Report opts for a division of tasks between the school boards that provide advice and support to the schools and a new administrative body, the Pedagogical Service, which monitors the self-evaluation process of the schools, reporting to the Ministry. In cases of poor evaluations, the Pedagogical Service could take measures ranging from providing assistance to reporting to authorities which can intervene directly. In this matter the Ministry of Education has decided to follow the suggestions resulting from QUESS.

It may be noted that reports and papers discussing the evaluation of school performance consider evaluations to be "a part of the school development process." With the minor exception of the report of the Committee on Education, they hardly ever refer to any kind of rewards or punishments brought about by the evaluations.

Recommendations resulting from QUESS and the Report of the Committee on Education have given rise to considerable public debate in North Rhine-Westfalia. What the outcome will be in terms of changes in education policy remains to be seen.

Bremen

Bremen is one of the two German Länder that have already changed their laws regarding education policies according to the principles of quality assurance. Schools have been made more autonomous, both administratively and financially.

The schools are required to develop school programs, in which they define their individuality, emphases, priorities, and goals. The school program is considered a work in progress, which is to be in a constant process of development. The school must set up a democratic structure for this purpose.

Schools evaluate themselves with reference to the framework set out in the school program. A new bureaucratic body, the School Inspection, was founded in order to conduct external evaluations of the schools. The School Inspection advises the schools in their development of school programs, and evaluates the schools' success in meeting the goals and standards set out in their school programs. It is speculated that this double role may lead to considerable tension between the autonomous school and the advising and evaluating School Inspection. The School Inspection is separate from the school boards and, unlike the school boards, it is not placed above the schools in the administrative hierarchy. The schools are not subjected to directives from the School Inspection, their relation is rather that of a partnership to ensure the quality of the schools.

Hessen

Like Bremen, Hessen has recently changed its education laws in the spirit of quality assurance. Hessen has gone much in the same direction as Bremen, but the changes have been more limited so far. The administrative structure remains mostly untouched. The schools are given partial autonomy, which cannot be limited "unnecessarily or without good reason" by the school board, as the law states.

According to the new education laws, all schools have to develop school programs and conduct self-evaluations. External evaluations are not required, but the school board can monitor schools, for example, by visiting classes and by participating in, and even calling, school council meetings. The school board assists the school in the development of the school program and oversees its implementation.

The recent education laws were passed with the remark that they were "an initiative to support the process of guiding the schools to greater autonomy." More changes in the same direction are expected to take place.

Saxony

The change in education law and the amalgamation of 20 national school boards and three secondary school boards into five regional school boards in Saxony have created administrative structures which in the long-term meet with the increased demands to secure educational responsibility even under increased quality requirements. The objective of the restructing process – in connection with the discussion on quality assurance – was to define new tasks or redefine old ones. The principal role of the regional school boards in their supervisory function is to advise and inspect schools. This means that schools are to be advised as far as their school development process is concerned so that they succeed in securing consistent, high-quality learning and school performance. In addition to visiting schools (as auditors), the school board staff, along with development organizers should support cooperation projects among schools, as well as encourage schools to become more open in their repective regions. Besides the board's advisory responsibility, the function of the school board is still, of course, to monitor schools, making sure that legal directives are carried out (education laws, school ordinances, administrative regulations including the curriculum and study plans, organizational directives, school-year scheduling, and other regulations).

School-level perspectives on accountability in Germany

Interviews were conducted in two schools. In the elementary level school (Grundschule), the Principal and four teachers participated in the interviews. The principal and two teachers from an academic secondary school (Gymnasium) also participated in the interviews.

Question 1: How do you understand the term accountability
in the context of your own school and classrooms?

Two-thirds of participants discussed their understanding of the term accountability largely in terms of their students. While some teachers mentioned their sense of responsibility towards their students and their success, several teachers highlighted their desire to encourage students to be accountable for their own learning. For example:

> "As a teacher, I lead the class but the students should also be partly accountable for the class. They often reject too much of their part.
> I try to lead the class with democratic methods and make the student thereby more accountable but it is difficult to get that point across to them."

Several teachers mentioned their sense of responsibility towards ensuring the safety of their students:

"We are accountable that the children are not harmed, and of course to educate them."

Two teachers also highlighted accountability in the context of the provision of social education for the students. They commented:

"In terms of social education, accountability is constantly transferred to us from society.
We now provide traffic, drug, health and sexual education."

One teacher also shared his/her sense of responsibility towards other teachers in the school:

"Teachers also belong to the school and they have to work well together. I am accountable to my colleagues."

Several teachers addressed the role of school policy and the need for the schools to meet the needs of all students. They elaborated:

"Accountability for school policy lies with the school committee which is comprised equally of parents and teachers.
We cannot teach all the children [of different ability and language backgrounds] the same thing, then both the weaker and the stronger students lose out. These are the obligations of the school. All children do not get the same thing, but each gets what is appropriate in each case."

One teacher understood accountability as a form of responsibility delegated by the state and by parents:

"First, we have accountability as prescribed by state laws. We are accountable for the children. We take over accountability from the parents. As the children are required by law to go to school, we take on accountability from the state."

Question 2: Who are your clients? Who are the other relevant stakeholders? What are some examples of their needs and wants?

The words used (especially the word "client") to ask this question provoked considerable response from interviewers who expressed a strong dislike of the use of business terminology in the context of schools. 80 percent of participants said they disliked the word client in discussions of the school and the school system. For example:

> "I am allergic to the word client. I don't think students are the clients of the teachers.
> The state minister of education speaks occasionally of students as clients. The school seeks to educate the students and does not want anything back from them, hence they are not the 'clients.'
> The school can be called a service business but there is no product. It is not possible to determine what the product is. It is not possible to speak of people in terms of good and bad products."

Two-thirds of respondents mentioned students as the most important objects of their accountability. These people felt accountability to prepare students for their future careers, to help them learn to work independently, and to ensure that schools were free from internal competition. For example:

> "We do not give any grades in the first two school years and in the third school year the parents decide if the children are given grades. I advise against it. We should try to keep competition out of the school."

The basic needs and wants of students were described by several teachers as "friendly teachers" who could be trusted, "good grades," "free time." Students also want "to learn something new."

Two-thirds of interviewees acknowledged the vested interest parents have in their child's education, their desire for information about their children's progress and their future potential. Two teachers also discussed parents' need for their children to be able to participate in the school's child care program. This program supplements daily school

170

hours and curriculum with additional supervised school time. It is designed to provide parents with daycare for their children. One teacher explained:

"Parents want and need daycare. We must offer this for the children because, for example, there are many single mothers who work. But, we get state funding for only ten children in the childcare program, but there are 40 children who use this service. The state should put more money into it. The parents should also contribute."

Several of those interviewed also named their colleagues as stakeholders in the educational process. Teachers discussed their need to be accountable to each other, their students and their parents. The need for teachers to work together and the challenges teachers are facing with respect to parental demands are reflected in these remarks:

"They are accountable with respect to each other, as a team. Teachers who teach the same subjects should communicate more with each other and be more of a team.
Teachers teach [more classes] and then they do not have as much time as they should to consult with parents. This arrangement often does not meet the needs of the parents."

Some participants also felt a sense of responsibility towards their schools, the community and greater society. As one teacher explained:

"Graduation is an intermediate goal, not the end goal. When students graduate they can go on to higher education. In that way, I have accountability towards the culture and society."

Question 3: What do you do at the present time that might be considered accountability?

Participants identified four of their current practices with accountability, the first of which concerned student social and academic growth. While most of these comments were made by elementary teachers, one secondary level participant also discussed his/her role in student growth initiatives. Building relationships with students and ensuring that students are building on their personal and academic skills were touted as key ingredients of teacher-based accountability. For example:

> "I evaluate where students stand and start from there.
> [To help students learn how to talk to each other, how to discuss things], we have a game-playing class when someone has a birthday. It is not just about game playing but interacting with each other. The children don't learn at home anymore. They have to be taught to interact and share."

Collaboration was a second form of teacher-identified accountability. One secondary teacher and two elementary teachers discussed their efforts to create collaborative liaisons with their colleagues. The form of this collaboration is exemplified in these comments:

> "We have pedagogy meetings. We discuss how we can make parent consultations more effective and meaningful. We have to advise the parents about what sort of high school their child should move on to."

School program planning was a third practice that respondents associated with accountability. The secondary school administrator and one of the school's teachers discussed their involvement in the development of their school programs.

> "My colleagues and I at the school have set up a discussion to develop the so-called 'school program.' It is mandated by the authorities. We discuss the pedagogical principles and accountability ... to whom are we accountable and how we can ensure accountability. We also discuss student behavior."

In relation to school-level autonomy and curricular decision-making, the teacher added:

"Schools have a certain freedom to determine their focus in terms of content and what subjects are offered at different stages."

Finally, both administrators pointed to their daily duties as part of their current efforts to be accountable.

"The principal is accountable both with respect to the children and to the teachers in the classroom. Educational guidelines and regulations must be followed up."

Question 4: What initiatives from the school district-level can you identify that seem to be aimed at increasing accountability?

None of the secondary school-level interviewers were able to identify accountability initiatives of the school district-level administration. But elementary-level respondents mentioned student evaluation, professional development, school planning, and child care initiatives. Elementary teachers indicated that their students do not receive grades until they enter third grade. At this time, it is up to the parents to decide if students will officially receive grades.

One teacher explained why grade three is the pivotal time to assign grades.

"At age ten (grade 4), students must move on in one of three different streams: Gymnasium, Realschule or Hauptschule. Gymnasium graduates go on to university. Realschule and Hauptschule usually go on to vocational training, internships or enter the job market."

One administrator commented on a renewed emphasis on professional development within the district and the school:

"Now we have one-day conferences where we can go deeper into pedagogical issues then in the short meetings."

Several elementary interviewees who identified school planning as an accountability-driven initiative focused their comments on the origin of school planning:

"The need for all schools to have a school program [plan] started from a district initiative.
The school plan defines what context the school works in and what its focus is. The application of what is laid out in the school plan is up to the individual."

Half of the elementary respondents discussed the impact of the child-care program and its ability to meet parental and student needs. As one teacher explained:

"This program [daycare offered from 8am to 1pm when parents are working and students are not in school] is very popular and is encouraged by the district. Although, it is up to the school to offer it."

Question 5: What initiative from the government-level can you identify that seem to be aimed at increasing accountability?

While half of the interviewees were unable to identify government-level accountability initiatives, the other half identified increasing school-level authority, student evaluation, and funding initiatives. In relation to increased school authority, one teacher noted:

"Schools have been given more autonomy, in organization, in pedagogy and even in allowing oral final examinations ... letting students graduate on passing oral final examinations."

In relation to school-level planning, one teacher mentioned:

"The main edict on the school is that the school has to be organized more clearly."

Throughout the interviews, there was a sense of increasing responsibility for the schools: parents increasingly wanted schools to assume responsibilities formerly assumed by the family.

Recent changes in curriculum were highlighted by several teachers as a government-sponsored tool designed to make schools more accountable. One teacher commented on curriculum reform as a return to the old ways.

"We now have to emphasize such things as spelling, mental arithmetic and learning poems by heart. Things that are out of fashion."

Finally, one of the elementary school interviewees, noting the impact of recent funding decreases by the government, claimed that "we have had to cut down on classes and increase their class sizes because we don't have enough teachers."

Switzerland

Background

Switzerland is comprised of 26 cantons or states, each with their own education system. Cantonal responsibilities include the development of their school system and individual school laws. The only exception is the federal law addressing maturity exams and vocational education. Accordingly, there is no federal education ministry. It is, therefore, impossible to present a unified picture of Swiss education policy, a problem encountered in other countries such as Germany and Canada. For this reason, this description of educational accountability in Switzerland remains necessarily general.

Several similar initiatives have been undertaken throughout the country. For example, over the last two decades there have been a series of curricular reform addressing mathematics and foreign language education. There also has been an increase in the number of foreign students who are participating in the education system. While the percentage of foreign students differs depending on the canton, all systems are attempting to adapt curricula to meet these changing conditions.

Each cantonal school system is guided by a nationally-endorsed philosophy supporting equal and equitable access for all eligible students. Students must begin school at age six. In nineteen cantons, students attend primary school for six years. While four cantons have implemented a four-year curriculum, three cantons have opted for a five-year primary education program.

The function and form of the lower secondary school is quite similar in each canton. Programs within these schools are usually offered at two levels and address either the basic or extended academic requirements. Each canton has different approaches to providing students with access to either stream of education. In some areas, both levels are taught in the same school. In others, different schools concern themselves with different curriculum.

Upper secondary school is one of two levels of education affected by federal law. In 1992, the federal government changed the regulations governing upper school-leaving examinations. The most significant policy change was that students were no longer required to select one of four specialized leaving examinations. It was recommended that all of the exams were compressed into one comprehensive assessment tool. This policy is still in the discussion stages in some cantons.

Accountability policies in Switzerland

School system management

All decisions about curriculum development priorities are decided at the upper levels of government, especially in French- and Italian-speaking cantons. But even in German Switzerland the Erziehungsrat has many priorities for the local commissions. Schools system management at the canton level is quite different across cantons. But at least some decision-making rests at this level, especially in respect to accountability. This is changing quickly with new definitions of roles and funtions for inspectors, head teachers, and others.

The local educational authority (commission scholaire) is comprised of elected members of the local community and members of the teaching staff. Many cantons have created additional levels of school system management. Two examples are the Erziehungsrat, an elected body that assists the government in its decision-making deliberations, and the Bezirksschulrat, a district-level administrative body. The most significant impact of this multi-layered and mostly elected form of governance is the time required to implement educational change.

In order to create a sense of unity between the cantonal systems, the Swiss Conference of Cantonal Directors of Education (SCCDE) was established. The Conference is comprised of four regional conferences. The Conference also administers several research-based institutions. The SCCDE also sets guidelines that determine the required entry age and duration of compulsory schooling in Switzerland. Within the Conference, the Pedagogical Commission is responsible for ensuring continuity in the resources available within the cantons.

Teaching training and professional development

In 1975, the SCCDE published "Teacher Training for Tomorrow." This document has served as the foundation for numerous reports on teacher training at each level of education.

Professional development is provided by a variety of sources. The SCCDE also coordinates the Swiss Center for In-Service Education of Secondary School Teachers. Several cantons administer training schools where experienced teachers may elect to study for six-month sessions, while receiving their full pay. But every canton has its own structures.

Within the elemantry schools and some secondary schools, teachers are evaluated by inspectors. The inspectors are either part-time members of the teaching staff, lay persons or members of the canton's educational staff. Several sources note that some cantons are discussing the implementation of salary-driven evaluation systems that would allow for either formal or self-evaluation.

Traditionally, teachers progress through one of two distinct teacher training programs. Upon completion of their compulsory studies, students progress through a four-year program at the Seminar. In the 1970s and 1980s, there were debates over the success of this format of teacher training. As a result, seminary training was increased to five to six years in duration. An additional form of teacher certification was developed. In this stream, students completing secondary school attend a two-year, university-based training program. Upper secondary school teachers must complete their subject-oriented university studies and then strengthen their pedagogical background. All Swiss cantons are presently changing their policies in order to implement studies A-levels and university studies. In the canton of Geneva, the initial professional training of primary teachers was completely transferred to the university (4 term study) in 1995.

Curriculum

Pedagogical and curricular development falls within the auspices of the cantonal authorities. Within the last several decades, all Swiss cantons have revised and revisited their curriculum. National curriculum coordination occurs by means of general recommendation around student achievement standards at each level of compulsory schooling. In 1992, a national statement on vocational school curriculum was issued by the SCCDE.

In most cases, curricular development is seen as a collaborative effort. Teachers are invited to participate in the process. Curricular reform usually entails a series of subject and grade level working groups.

Teachers, both nationally and cantonally, have a large degree of freedom. Although their pedagogical choices are not limited by specific guidelines, certain textbooks are used within the canton. Certain cantons have begun to place emphasis on group-based and specialized individual learning strategies.

Student evaluation

In most cases, students receive two or three written evaluations a year, particularly in elementary schools. Within many cantons, the traditional numerical system of primary student assessment has been replaced with a more observational method of evaluation.

Student selection and progression practices vary from canton to canton. Decisions regarding a student's admissibility to an academic secondary school are often based on past performance, teacher evaluation and parental desire. Within secondary schools, there is a national certification examination upon completion of apprenticeship programs. The academic secondary programs include a final examination after which students receive their Matura certificate. It is this certificate which allows students to apply to university programs.

In 1995, the Committee adapted the Matura regulations in order to promote independent student learning. As a result, students have been permitted to select specializations within the nine established disciplines. It is the hope of the Committee that this program will be adopted by all cantons by 2003.

Research and development

Switzerland has a long tradition of educational research. The Swiss Society for Research in Education (SSRE) completed the "Development Plan for Educational Research in Switzerland." Between 1991 and 1997, the national research program conducted a study entitled, "The Efficiency of our Education and Training System." In another attempt to support national and cantonal research efforts, the National Coordination and Conference for Education Research Policy was established in 1992. This body enables national and cantonal administrators and educators to conduct collaborative research programs.

School-level perspectives on accountability in Switzerland

This section describes the results of interviews with a small number of staff members, from a "convenience" sample of just two schools, about the their understandings of accountability and their views of accountability initiatives in their country and school.

Interviews with nine school practitioners were conducted in two schools. At the secondary school, the principal and two teachers were interviewed. Participants at the elementary school included the principal and four members of the teaching staff.

Question 1: How do you understand the term accountability in the context of your own school and classroom?

Students were mentioned as a key client group by all of the secondary school respondents. Their sense of accountability for students is reflected in these comments:

> "Success for those who graduate from our school is measured by the pupil's ability to find a job. Their physical, mental and psychological development during their education at our school [is also an informal way of interpreting the level of student success]. Assisting them in attaining an excellent development of their skills is also our role.
> We have to make sure our graduates are equipped with the necessary skills for the next school level."

When discussing their perception of accountability at the school level, one teacher added the responsibility of "creating a human atmosphere and climate within the school."

Teachers and administrators at both schools unanimously listed teaching as a key element of their understanding of school-based accountability. Their own personal evaluation of the quality of their teaching was seen as an essential component of their accountability:

> "The constant development and adjustment of teaching styles and

goals ... and the exchange and conversation between teachers ... is an important [element of accountability].

I understand accountability in the sense that third persons should have an inside view in my daily work. In doing so, they are able to reflect on my work and give me feedback on issues about which I am not conscious."

One teacher also identified his/her sense of responsibility to society and the community:

"Accountability for me implies that I am aware of my responsibility towards the society for whom I am producing a certain service."

Question 2: Who are your clients and other relevant stakeholders? What are some example of their needs and wants?

Interviewees made clear distinctions between client and stakeholder groups. They also clearly delineated client and stakeholder needs and wants. Four distinct groups of clients and stakeholders were identified.

All but one participant mentioned students as the primary clients of the school and school system but only the secondary staff pointed to parents as clients.

One elementary teacher emphasized the role of the student as client and stressed that, "all students, including those with special needs, are important [clients]."

With respect to student needs and wants, respondents noted:

"Good education that will enable students to find a job after school. Education in the larger sense ... not just teaching ... but AIDS, drugs, sex and prevention.
[We are also responsible for providing a] good school climate and identification with the school and attention to the individual child's needs."

Parents were the most frequently mentioned stakeholders in schools and school systems. Interviewees' comments varied depending on their primary or secondary level affiliation. While secondary staff identified parents as clients, elementary staff named parents as stakeholders in the educational process. The greater family unit was also highlighted by elementary teachers as an important stakeholder group. Teachers and administrators stressed the importance of two-way communication with parents, and parental knowledge of school activities and student progress.

Secondary school teachers, and the elementary school administrator, also felt that cantonal administration, the school board and future employers were stakeholders in the school.

Future employers, social service agencies, medical professionals, academic institutions, and society in general were all listed by individual participants as groups with a vested interest in the educational system.

Question 3: What do you do at the present time
that might be considered accountability?

Teachers and administrators commented on several initiatives that were designed to increase teacher accountability. Their comments dealt with teacher/teacher collaboration and principal/teacher evaluation. For example, the elementary principal explained:

> "We have developed a new mechanism, the 'accountability dialogue,' between the principal and the teacher that will be working from winter 1998. During the accountability dialogue, teacher and principal will sit together to evaluate their work on three levels 1) teaching 2) the school 3) teacher's personal situation."

In addition, several teachers commented on the importance of "respecting the duties of the teaching program," and "comparing their classes with those of their colleagues."

> "Organizing conferences between teachers exchanging opinions and teaching material [is an important accountability initiative]."

Secondary teachers and administrators unanimously agreed that "communication between students and teachers" was a key feature of their accountability efforts. While student evaluation was mentioned by only one participant, several participants provided a more holistic approach. For example, both secondary and elementary participants discussed the importance of, "encouraging the pupil's self-confidence and sense of responsibility."

Communication and collaboration were also seen as important elements of their parent-focused accountability initiatives. Feedback sessions with parents to discuss student progress, and several other parent/teacher events were mentioned by participants at both levels. Reporting school-based activities, including an annual report in the newspaper, was highlighted by two elementary school teachers.

Question 4: What initiatives from the district-level can you identify that seem to be aimed at increasing accountability?

In response to this question, several teachers discussed the pending legislation to be introduced in 1999 and expressed the belief that it will have a great impact on teaching and their school. Addressing the same issue, two teachers mentioned the sense of insecurity and anticipation their colleagues have about the new legislation. Addressing the nature of this legislation, one participant added,

> "They have asked us to develop guidelines for accountability and to produce a list with all the obligations of our teachers. We know that we will be under a greater external control."

The school commission was also identified as a district-level accountability mechanism:

> "The school commission visits us from time to time. That is they assist during a lesson. This form of accountability has always been in place. It does not have a huge impact because a high standard of excellence is constantly maintained."

Another teacher added:

"Sometimes the school commission produces intelligent and constructive criticism or proposals which we have to take into account."

Conclusion

A very high proportion of reform initiatives over the past 15 years have aimed to increase the accountability of schools and school systems. Evidence from a review of such initiatives suggests that this same basic aim can be met in many different ways depending, in part, on the assumptions one holds about the nature of schools, the extent to which they are responding adequately to society's needs, and how best they can be changed.

Most countries examined for this study were very eclectic with respect to their approaches to accountability. When only the tools for accountability are considered, such eclecticism appears harmless, perhaps even to be desired. But when the underlying assumptions associated with these tools are taken into account, eclecticism seems more likely to sow the seeds of confusion and loss of support on the part of those who must implement the tools or provide the account. "Am I considered to be a responsible professional simply in need of greater authority and flexibility? Or am I considered to be a marginally competent worker in need of extrinsic rewards and punishments in order to do an adequate job?" Are schools basically effective institutions that can become even more effective with some clearer direction and planning? Or are they lazy, unresponsive organizations that need to be radically transformed?

Policy-makers approaching the selection of accountability would do well to consider explicitly the assumptions underlying their instruments of choice. They would do well, also, to weigh the strengths and weaknesses of selecting a repertoire of tools that share the same basic assumptions about schools and schooling.

Summary

Section A

The first main section of the report accomplishes three goals. First, it provides some background to help understand the timing and reasons for the substantial initiatives undertaken worldwide to increase educational accountability. Calls for such an increase began in many countries in the mid 1960s and gained considerable momentum during the mid to late 1980s. Although the timing of such calls for greater educational accountability was common to many countries, the reasons giving rise to these calls were rooted in the particular economic, political and social contexts of those countries. These roots potentially are the source of considerable variation in approaches to accountability. But because many countries share a New Right political context, this variation is more muted than would otherwise be expected.

A second goal of this section is to clarify the meaning of accountability. This is accomplished through a liberal adaptation of Walkers (1989) philosophical analysis of accountability relationships and their moral adequacy. From this analysis, we propose that accountability approaches and tools can be distinguished by the nature of their response to five issues: who is to be held accountable, to whom the account is owed, what is to be accounted for, what is the level of accountability called for, and what are the consequences of providing the account.

Section A also describes four major approaches to accountability: market-oriented approaches, decentralization of decision-making approaches, professionalization approaches, and managerial approaches. Each of these approaches is built on a unique set of basic beliefs and assumptions about schools and how they can be changed, and each draws on a unique set of accountability tools. These four approaches serve as a framework for a more detailed description of accountability tools in Section B of the report.

Section B

This section of the report describes a large number of quite specific tools used to increase the accountability of schools, school districts and larger educational jurisdictions, such as provinces, states and nations. These tools encompass most of the "reform" and "restructuring" initiatives that have been advocated for education over the past decade, reminding us that accountability has been the preeminent goal for educational reformers during this period. Accountability tools described in this section emerge from the four distinctly different approaches to accountability summarized in Section A. In the case of each approach, this section reviews and extends its underlying assumptions and describes examples of specific accountability tools associated with each approach.

Market approaches to accountability increase the competition among schools and districts for students. They do this on the assumption that monopolistic organizations are neither efficient nor sensitive to the needs of their clients. Opening school and district boundaries, privatizing schools, and developing schools with specialized missions are among the tools used as part of this approach to accountability. In conjunction with more flexible allocation of funding (e.g., vouchers, tuition tax credits) these tools allow parents and students to "exit" schools with which they are dissatisfied and find schools more to their liking. Publicly ranking schools using aggregated student achievement scores, another tool associated with the market approach, provides parents and students information to help inform their choices.

186

A second approach to accountability is decentralization of decision-making authority and the tools associated with this approach are several forms of site-based management. One of the central aims of decentralization is to increase the voice of those who are not heard (or at least not sufficiently listened to) in the context of typical school governance structures. The assumption in this case is that "exit" is not the only means of giving parents more power in shaping their childrens' school experiences. Another option is to give parents and students more "voice" in improving the school to which children are assigned in a non-choice context. When this is the goal, community control forms of site-based management are the tools used for its achievement.

Decentralization of decision-making authority, however, is sometimes rooted in a broader reform strategy for public institutions, generally, which is referred to as "new managerialism." In countries where school reform has been substantially influenced by new managerialism, the underlying assumption is that public institutions, schools included, are inefficient and not generally cost-effective. Administrative control forms of site-based management are considered to be effective tools for ameliorating these shortcomings.

There are two radically different accountability strategies that have a professional orientation. One of these approaches manifests itself most obviously in the implementation of professional-control models of school-based management. The other approach encompasses the standards movement as it applies to the practices of teachers and administrators. What both strategies hold in common is a belief in the central contribution of professional practice in schools to their outcomes. The strategies differ most obviously on which practices they chose for their direct focus: in the case of professional control school-based management, the focus is on school-level decision-making whereas teachers' classroom instructional and curricular practices are the focus of the standards movement.

Not to be confused with "new managerialism," managerial approaches to accountability include systematic efforts to create more goal-oriented, efficient and effective schools by introducing systematic management procedures. A fundamental assumption underlying this approach to accountability is that there is nothing fundamentally wrong with current school structures. Nevertheless, their effectiveness and efficiency will be improved to the extent that they become more strategic in their choices of goals, and more planful and data-driven about the means used to accomplish those goals. "Cost effectiveness," and "value added" are phrases that capture the mission of those advocating management approaches to accountability, and "control," in its various forms, is the mechanism for accomplishing this mission. Tools associated with managerial approaches to accountability differ in what it is they aim to control (one or more of the inputs, processes, and outputs of schooling), and how that control is exercised.

Section C

Building on the concepts and ideas developed in the two earlier sections of the report, the third and final section examines accountability policies and practices in eight countries. These countries include Scotland, The Netherlands, Norway, New Zealand, Canada (the province of Ontario), Hungary, Germany, and Switzerland.

In the case of each country, a non-exhaustive sample of accountability policies or tools are reviewed. This further clarifies the nature of many of the tools described in Section B. It also begins to reflect the state-of-the-art of accountability practices at the present time.

In addition, this section reports the results of interviewing approximately five staff members (the principal and four teachers) in each of two schools in each country. These interviews capture some of the perspectives held by those in schools about the meaning of accountability, how accountability is reflected in their own school contexts, and how district and government accountability policies are viewed. These interviews are not intended as an evaluation of accountability policies. Nor are they intended to comprehensively "represent" the views of those working in schools. Rather, the results of the interviews put a human face on accountability policies, and illustrate some of the important differences in perspectives that need to be bridged for policy to influence practice.

188

References

Amos, N., & Cheeseman, R. (1992). *Provisional teachers failing the Mississippi teacher assessment instruments for certification: An evaluation for 1991–1992.* Paper presented at the annual meeting of the Mid-South Educational Research Association, Knoxville, Tennessee.

Apple, M.W. (1996). *Cultural politics and education.* New York: Teachers College Press.

Black, P.J. (1994). Performance assessment and accountability: The experience in England and Wales. *Educational Evaluation and Policy Analysis, 16*(2), 191–203.

Briseid, O. (1995). *Comprehensive Reform in Upper Secondary Education in Norway: a retrospective view. European Journal of Education,* Vol. 30(3).

Bryk, A.S., & Hermanson, K. (1993). Educational indicator systems: Observations on their structure, interpretation, and use. In *Review of research in education, volume 19* (pp. 451–484). Washington: American Educational Research Association.

Bullock, A., & Thomas, H. (1997). *Schools at the center? A study of decentralization.* London: Routledge.

Butterworth, G. & Butterworth, S. (1998). Reforming Education: The New Zealand Experience, 1984–1996. Palmerston North: Dunmore Press.

Caldas, S.J., & Mossavat, M.K. (1994). *A statewide program assessment survey of parents', teachers', and principals' perceptions of school report cards*. Paper presented at the annual meeting of the American Educational Research Association, New Orleans.

Canadian Education Statistics Council (1996). *Education indicators in Canada*. Toronto: Canadian Education Statistics Council.

Carlson, R. (1965). Barriers to change in public schools. In R. Carlson et al. (Eds.), *Change processes in the public schools*. Eugene, OR: University of Oregon, Center for the Advanced Study of Educational Administration.

Carroll, S., & Walford, G. (1997). Parents' responses to the school quasi-market. *Research Papers in Education: Policy and Practice, 12*(1), 3–26.

Committee on Education and Labor (1993). *Goals 2000: Educate America*. Washington, DC: U.S. House of Representatives, 103rd Congress, 1st Session.

Conley, S., & Odden, A. (1995). Linking teacher compensation to teacher career development. *Educational Evaluation and Policy Analysis, 17*(2), 219–237.

Cookson, P.W. (1992). The rise of the school choice movement. *Educational Policy, 6*(2), 99–104.

Darling-Hammond, L. (1989). Teaching supply, demand, and standards. *Educational Policy, 3*(1), 1–17.

Darling-Hammond, L. (1992). Educational indicators and enlightened policy. *Educational Policy, 6*(3), 235–265.

Darling-Hammond, L., Falk, B., & Ancess, L. (1995). *Authentic assessment in action: Studies of schools and students*. New York: Teachers College Press.

Davis, O.L. (1998). National and state curriculum standards: Reasonable conequences, possible prospects. *Journal of Curriculum and Supervision, 13*(4), 297–299.

Doerr, E., et al. (1996). *The case against school vouchers*. Amherst, NY: Prometheus Books.

Dunn, D. (1994). *Charter schools: Experiments in reform*. Report prepared for the Texas State Legislative Budget Board, Austin, Texas.

Dwyer, C.A. (1994). Criteria for performance-based teacher assessments: Validity, standards, and issues. *Journal of Personnel Evaluation in Education, 8*, 135–150.

190

Ellwein, M.C., & Glass, G. (1991). Testing for competence: Translating reform policy into practice. *Educational Policy, 5*(1), 64–78.

Erickson, R., et al. (1995). *State special education outcomes: A report on how states are assessing educational outcomes for students with disabilities.* Minneapolis, MN: National Center on Educational Outcomes.

Finn, C.E. (1996). *Different schools for a better future.* Indianapolis, IN: Hudson Institute.

Finn, C.E., & Ravitch, D. (1995). *Education reform, 1994–1995.* Indianapolis, IN: Hudson Institute.

Firestone, W.A., Mayrowetz, D., & Fairman, J. (1998). Performance-based assessment and instructional change: The effects of testing in Maine and Maryland. *Educational Evaluation and Policy Analysis, 20*(2), 95–113.

Florida Department of Education (1991). *Blueprint 2000.* Florida: State Legislature Report.

Fullan, M. (1992). *Successful school improvement.* Buckingham, UK: Open University Press.

Gamoran, A. (1996). Student achievement in public magnet, public comprehensive, and private city high schools. *Educational Evaluation and Policy Analysis, 18*(1), 1–18.

Glasman, N., & Heck, R. (1996). Chapter 12: Role-based evaluation of principals. In K. Leithwood et al. (Eds.), *International handbook of educational leadership and administration* (pp. 369–394). Netherlands: Kluwer Academic Publishers.

Hanson, E.M. (1992). Educational marketing and the public schools: Policies, practices, and problems. *Educational Policy, 6*(1), 19–34.

Hargreaves, A. (1991). Contrived collegiality. In J. Blase (Ed.), *The politics of school life.* San Francisco, CA: Sage.

Hargreaves, A., et al. (1990). *The management of development planning – A paper for local education authorities.* London: DES.

Hausman, C., et al. (1997). *Organizational capacity for school improvement: Teacher reports in magnet and nonmagnet schools.* Paper presented at the annual meeting of the American Educational Research Association, Chicago.

Heneman, R., & Ledford, G. (1998). Competency pay for professionals and managers in business: A review and implications for teachers. *Journal of Personnel Evaluation in Education, 12*(2), 103–121.

Hogan, D. (1992). "... the silent compulsions of economic relations": Markets and the demand for education. *Educational Policy, 6*(2), 180–205.

Howell, J.F. (1995). *Using profiles to improve schools*. Paper presented at the annual meeting of the American Educational Research Association, San Francisco.

How good is our school? Her Majesty's Inspector of Schools, The Scottish Office Edinburgh (1996).

Interstate New Teacher Assessment and Support Consortium (1992). *Model standards for beginning teacher licensing, assessment and development: A resource for state dialogue*. Mimeo.

Interstate New Teacher Assessment and Support Consortium (n.d.). *Model standards in mathematics for beginning teacher licensing and development: A resource for state dialogue*. Mimeo.

Kotler, P., & Andreasen, A. (1987). *Strategic marketing for nonprofit organizations, third edition*. Englewood Cliffs, NJ: Prenticehall.

Lange, C.M. (1997). *Charter schools and special education: A handbook*. Alexandria, VA: National Association of State Directors of Special Education.

Leithwood, K. (1998). Educational governance and student achievement. *Orbit, 29*(1), 34–37.

Leithwood, K., & Aitken, R. (1995). *Making schools smarter*. Thousand Oaks, CA: Corwin Press.

Linn, R.L. (1987). Accountability: The comparison of educational systems and the quality of test results. *Educational Policy, 1*(2), 181–198.

Louis, K.S., & Kruse, S. (1995). *Professionalism and community: Perspectives on reforming urban schools*. Thousand Oaks, CA: Corwin Press.

Louis, K.S., & Miles, M. (1992). *Improving the urban high school: What works and why*. London: Cassell.

MacGilchrist, B., et al. (1995). *Planning matters: The impact of development planning in primary schools*. London: Paul Chapman Publishing Ltd.

Madsen, J. (1996). *Private and public school partnerships: Sharing lessons about decentralization.* London: Falmer Press.

Mager, R.F. (1972). *Goal analysis.* Belmont, CA: Fearon Publishers.

Making it Happen in Twelve Schools. Her Majesty's Inspector of Schools, The Scottish Office Edinburgh (1996).

Marsh, D. (1997). *School reform and decentralization in the United States: The national alliance experience.* Paper presented at the annual meeting of the American Educational Research Association, Chicago.

McEwen, N., & Chow, H. (1991). Issues in implementing indicator systems. *Alberta Journal of Educational Research, 37*(1), 65–86.

Meier, D.W. (1997). Can the odds be changed? *Educational Policy, 11*(2), 194–208.

Melnick, S., & Pullin, D. (1987). Testing teachers' professional knowledge: Legal and educational policy implications. *Educational Policy, 1*(2), 215–228.

Mestinsek, R. (1993). District and school profiles for quality education. *Alberta Journal of Educational Research, 39*(2), 179–189.

Mintzberg, H. (1994). *The rise and fall of strategic planning.* New York: The Free Press.

Mohrman, A.M., Mohrman, S.A., & Odden, A. (1996). Aligning teacher compensation with systemic school reform: Skill-based pay and group-based performance rewards. *Educational Evaluation and Policy Analysis, 18*(1), 51–71.

Nathan, J. (1996). Possibilities, problems, and progress: Early lessons from the charter movement. *Phi Delta Kappan, 78*(1), 18–23.

Nathan, J. (1998). Heat and light in the charter school movement *Phi Delta Kappan, 79*(7), 499–505.

National Board for Professional Teaching Standards (1998). Webpage information, available at nbpts. org.

Neil, M., et al. (1995). *Implementing performance assessment: A guide to classroom, school, and system reform.* Cambridge, MA: Fair Test.

Nelson, M.D., & Bauch, P.A. (1997). *African-American students' perceptions of caring teacher behaviors in Catholic and public schools of choice.* Paper presented at the annual meeting of the American Educational Research Association, Chicago.

New Zealand Government (n.d.). *Educational Review Office* <http://www.ero.govt.nz/about/index.htm> (1998, July 14).

New Zealand Government (n.d.). *New Zealand Qualification Services.* <http://www.nzqa.govt.nz/services/services.html> (1998, July 8).

New Zealand Ministry of Education: *Te tahulu o te matauranga (1998, April 30.). Draft Framework of Professional Standards.* <http://www.minedu.govt.nz/schools/professional standards/consult.htm> (1998, July 31).

New Zealand Ministry of Education: *Te tahulu o te matauranga (1998, July 9). Standards for Teacher Education.* <http://www. minedu.govt. nz/teacher/review97/finalsubs/intro.htm> (1998, July 31).

New Zealand Ministry of Education: *Te tahulu o te matauranga (1998, May). Green Paper: Assessment for Success.* <http://www. minedu. govt.nz/schools/primary/assessment/exec.htm> (1998, July 31).

New Zealand Ministry of Education: *Te tahulu o te matauranga (n.d.). Board of Trustees.* <http://www.minedu.govt.nz/schools/BoT> (1998, July 31).

New Zealand Ministry of Education: *Te tahulu o te matauranga (n.d.). Education in the 21st Century.* <http://www.minedu.govt.nz/ed21> (1998, July 31).

New Zealand Ministry of Education: *Te tahulu o te matauranga (n.d.). Schooling in New Zealand: A Guide.* <http://www.minedu.govt.nz/schools/guide> (1998, July 31).

New Zealand Ministry of Education: *Te tahulu o te matauranga (n.d.). Teacher Registration Board.* <htpp://www.minedu.govt.nz/schools/ /BoT/part1_7.htm> (1998, July 31).

New Zealand Ministry of Education: *Te tahulu o te matauranga (n.d.). The New Zealand Curriculum Framework.* <http://www.minedu.govt. nz/curriculum/nzcf/frame.htm> (1998, July 31).

Newmann, F., Brandt, R., & Wiggins, G. (1998). An exchange of views on "semantics, psychometrics, and assessment reform: A close look at 'authentic' assessments." *Educational Researcher, 27*(6), 19–22.

No Author (1992). Guidelines for designing a school profile.

No Author (1994). *District and school profiles for quality education.* Alberta: Grande Prairie Public School District.

Norwegian Royal Ministry of Education, Research and Church Affairs

(1996, October 10). *The Compulsory School Reform.* <odin.dep.
no/kuf/publ/gr97/96nr04e.html>. (1998, July 10).

Norwegian Royal Ministry of Education, Research and Church Affairs
(1996, October 18). *The Development of Education from 1994–96:
Norway-National Report.* <odin.dep/kuf/publ/highed>. (1998, July
10).

Norwegian Royal Ministry of Education, Research and Church Affairs
(1998, March 27). *Information dossiers on the structures of the
education systems in Europe: Norway 1997.* <odin.dep.no/kuf/publ/
dice>. (1998, July 3).

Oakes, J. (1989). What educational indicators? The case for assessing
the school context. *Educational Evaluation and Policy Analysis,
11*(2), 181–199.

Paris, D.C. (1998). Standards and charters: Horace Mann meets Tinker
Bell. *Educational Policy, 12*(4), 380–396.

Peters, M. (1992). Performance indicators in New Zealand higher
education: Accountability or control? *Journal of Education Policy,
7*(3), 267–283.

Porter, A.C. (1991). Creating a system of school process indicators.
Educational Evaluation and Policy Analysis, 13(1), 13–29.

Pounder, D.G., & Young, P. (1996). Chapter 9: Recruitment and selection of educational administrators. In K. Leithwood et al. (Eds.),
International handbook of educational leadership and administration
(pp. 279–308). Netherlands: Kluwer Academic Publishers.

Premack, E. (1996). Charter schools: California's education reform
"power tool." *Phi Delta Kappan, 78*(1), 60–64.

Rafferty, E.A., & Treff, A.V. (1994). School-by-school test score comparisons: Statistical issues and pitfalls. *ERS Spectrum, 12*(2), 16–19.

Ratteray, J.D. (1997). *How much is too much? Charters, vouchers, and
corporate philanthropy.* Washington, DC: Institute for Independent
Education, Inc.

Raywid, M. (1992). Choice orientations, discussions, and prospects.
Educational Policy, 6(2), 105–122.

Rehfuss, J. (1995). Privatization in education. *Research Roundup,
11*(3).

Riley, K., & Nuttall, D. (Eds.) (1994). *Measuring quality: Education indicators in the United Kingdom and international perspectives.* London: The Falmer Press.

Ritzen, J.M., et al. (1997). School finance and school choice in the Netherlands. *Economics of Education Review, 16*(3), 329–335.

Saks, J.B. (1997). The voucher debate: Should public money follow kids to private schools? *American School Board Journal, 184*(3), 24–28.

Schneider, B., Schiller, K.S., & Coleman, J. (1996). Public school choice: Some evidence from the National Education Longitudinal study of 1988. *Educational Evaluation and Policy Analysis, 18*(1), 19– 29.

Schwartz, P. (1991). *The art of the long view.* New York: Doubleday.

Scriven, M. (1994). Duties of the teacher. *Journal of Personnel Evaluation in Education, 8*, 151–184.

Smithson, J.L., et al. (1995). *Describing the enacted curriculum: Development and dissemination of opportunity to learn indicators in science education.* Paper commissioned by the SCASS Science Project.

Southwest Educational Development Lab (1995). *Redefining educational governance: The charter school concept.* Austin, TX: SEDL.

Stoll, L., & Fink, D. (1992). Effecting school change: The Halton approach. *School Effectiveness and School Improvement, 3*(1), 19–41.

Terwilliger, J. (1998). Rejoinder: Response to Wiggins and Newman. *Educational Researcher, 27*(6), 22–23.

The Role of School Development Plans in Managing School Effectiveness. Her Majesty's Inspector of Schools, The Scottish Office Edinburgh (1994).

The Scottish Office (1997, September). *The Curriulum in Secondary Schools 1997–98.* <www.scotland.gov.uk/news/relesase98_1/pr1343.htm> (1998, July 14).

The Scottish Office (1998, June 30). *Summary Results of the 1997–98 School Census.* <www.scotland.gov.uk/news/relesase98_1/pr1315.htm> (1998, July 14).

The Scottish Office (1998, March 14). *Draft Guidelines for Initial Teacher Education Courses in Scotland.* <www.scotland.gov.uk/frame21.htm> (1998, July 14).

196

Tyler, R.W. (1949). *Basic principles of curriculum and instruction.* Chicago, IL: University of Chicago Press.

Urbanski, A. (1998). Teacher professionalism and teacher accountability: Toward a more genuine teaching profession. *Educational Policy, 12*(4), 449–457.

Vanourek, G., et al. (1997). *Charter school as seen by those who know them best: Students, teachers, and parents.* Indianapolis, IN: Hudson Institute.

Walberg, H.J. (1990). OECD indicators of educational productivity. *Educational Researcher, 19*(5), 30–33.

Whitty, G. (1997). Creating quasi-markets in education. In M.W. Apple (Ed.), *Review of research in education, volume 22* (pp. 3–47). Washington, DC: American Educational Research Association.

Willms, J.D., & Kerckhoff, A. (1995). The challenge of developing new educational indicators. *Educational Evaluation and Policy Analysis, 17*(1), 113–131.

Wise, A.E., & Leibrand, J. (1996). Profession-based accreditation: A foundation for high-quality teaching. *Phi Delta Kappan, 78*(3), 202–206.

Witte, J.F. (1992). Public subsidies for private schools: What we know and how to proceed. *Educational Policy, 6*(2), 206–227.

Wohlstetter, P., & Buffett, T. (1992). Decentralizing dollars under school-based management: Have policies changed? *Educational Policy, 6*(1), 35–54.

Yu, C.M., & Taylor, W. (1997). *Difficult choices: Do magnet schools serve children in need?* Report of the Citizens' Commission on Civil Rights.

The Authors

Kenneth Leithwood Professor and Head, Center for Leadership Development, OISE/University of Toronto. Specializes in leadership, organizational design, and school improvement processes.

Karen Edge Doctoral student, OISE/University of Toronto. Spezializes in higher education policy issues.

Doris Jantzi Senior Research Associate, Center for Leadership Development, OISE/University of Toronto. Spezializes in leadership, policy analysis, and quantative data analysis.

DATE DUE